A KEY TO THE ADULTS
OF THE BRITISH EPHEMEROPTERA

Emerging male imago of *Ecdyonurus venosus* (Photo: M. Mizzaro).

A KEY TO THE ADULTS

OF THE BRITISH

EPHEMEROPTERA

with notes on their ecology

by

J. M. ELLIOTT

Freshwater Biological Association

and

U. H. HUMPESCH

Limnological Institute,
Austrian Academy of Sciences

Illustrated by

Prof. M. Mizzaro-Wimmer
Zoological Institute, University of Vienna

D. E. Kimmins
Formerly of the British Museum: Natural History

and

J. M. Elliott

FRESHWATER BIOLOGICAL ASSOCIATION
SCIENTIFIC PUBLICATION No. 47

1983

Published by the Freshwater Biological Association, The Ferry House,
Ambleside, Cumbria   LA22 oLP
© Freshwater Biological Association 1983

ISBN 0 900386 45 2
ISSN 0367-1887

PREFACE

The Association's first key to British Ephemeroptera, written by Mr D. E. Kimmins, was published in 1942 and included keys to the families and genera of nymphs. These were omitted when a new revised key to adults was published in 1954, with a second edition in 1972. A separate key to nymphs, written by Dr T. T. Macan, was published in 1961, with second and third editions in 1970 and 1979.

Some of the excellent illustrations from the earlier key to adults are included in the present publication but more illustrations have been added and the text has been completely rewritten. The section on adult ecology has been greatly expanded – some of the information coming from the authors' own researches. The list of references has also been enlarged to contain all the more important publications known to the authors.

We have been fortunate in having two authors to revise and expand this key who have researched on various aspects of ephemeropteran natural history both independently and in collaboration. Dr Humpesch brings his experience of the taxonomy and ecology of the Ephemeroptera in continental Europe to bear on the same problems in Britain and this has enhanced the value of this revision.

Imitation of 'duns' and 'spinners' exercises the ingenuity of fly-fishermen. The trout that they attempt to entice with these imitations have often grown on a diet to which ephemeropterans have made a substantial contribution. As the second half of this handbook describes, the Ephemeroptera have fascinating life-histories and behaviour that are of much interest to entomologists and freshwater biologists. I hope that all these readers will welcome this new key in the Association's series.

The Ferry House
September 1983

E. D. Le Cren
Director

CONTENTS

INTRODUCTION

Ephemeroptera belong to the Exopterygota (or Hemimetabola), i.e. those insects with an incomplete metamorphosis, with a larva that basically resembles the adult in appearance, with wings that develop externally as wing buds in the immature stages, and with a life cycle divided into three definite stages of egg, larva and adult. The name Ephemeroptera (Greek *ephēmeros* = lasting for a day; *pteron* = wing) refers to the brief life of the adult, which is sometimes called a 'mayfly' or 'one-day fly'. Adults do not feed, and live for only one or two hours in some species but up to about fourteen days in some ovoviviparous species. Ephemeroptera are unique among winged insects in having two adult stages. The first, called the *subimago*, emerges from the last larval stage and, depending on air temperature, usually moults within 24 hours to the second, called the *imago* (plural *imagines*). Fishermen usually refer to the subimago as the dun and the imago as the spinner. Larvae are also called nymphs or naiads by some workers.

Linnaeus originally placed ephemeropterans in the Neuroptera, together with all insects with net-veined wings. This miscellany of insects was gradually split into several orders, including the Ephemeroptera. It is a small order with just over 2000 species, about 200 genera and 19 families. Fossil evidence suggests that the order was once richer in species. The earliest fossils from Lower Permian beds differ from present-day Ephemeroptera in having both pairs of wings of about equal size and all three pairs of legs long and slender. The hind wings are reduced in some Jurassic fossils, and adults similar to those of present-day families have been found in the Baltic Amber of the Tertiary (Eocene, or Lower or Middle Oligocene). Edmunds & Traver (1954) proposed that the Ephemeroptera were derived from lepismatoid insects (bristle-tails).

The key to adults in the present publication is partially based on earlier keys by Kimmins (1942, 1972). As adult females sometimes cannot be identified to species, some authors have tried to use egg morphology as a taxonomic characteristic (Degrange 1960; Koss 1968; Kopelke & Müller-Liebenau 1981a, b, 1982; Malzacher 1982). A key to nymphs (larvae) of the British species and notes on their ecology can be found in Macan (1979). The general biology of Ephemeroptera was reviewed by Illies (1968) and more recent literature has been reviewed by Brittain (1982). Information on the life cycles of 297 species has been summarized by Clifford (1982).

GENERAL CHARACTERS

The basic external structure of the adult is illustrated in fig. 1. The most important structural characters are the wings, including their venation and the presence or absence of hind wings, the number of long caudal filaments or "tails" at the hind end of the abdomen, the number of tarsal segments in the legs, the structure of the male genitalia, and the colour pattern on the wings and abdomen. Subimagines are usually easy to separate from imagines because their colours are duller and their wings are fringed with hairs which are absent in all imagines except those in the family Caenidae.

Head. The antennae are very short with two segments (a short basal *scapus* and a longer *pedicellus*) and a terminal bristle. There are one median and two lateral *ocelli*, and compound eyes that are much larger in males than in females. Males of some Baetidae and Leptophlebiidae have turbinate eyes, i.e. the eye is divided, with the upper part raised on a stalk-like or turret-like portion. The mouth parts are vestigial and non-functional.

Thorax and legs. There are three regions of the thorax: anterior *prothorax* with the fore legs, *mesothorax* with the middle pair of legs and the fore wings, posterior *metathorax* with the hind legs and hind wings (may be absent). The fore legs usually differ in the sexes, those of the male being much longer than those of the female and also longer than the middle and hind legs of both sexes. Each leg has six parts: a stout basal *coxa*, a small *trochanter*, a large flattened *femur*, a slender cylindrical *tibia*, a slender cylindrical *tarsus* and apical *claws*. The tarsus (part of the leg next to the claws) has five, four or three free segments, one or two segments being fused to the tibia in the latter cases. There are two tarsal claws, sometimes dissimilar in form.

Wings. There are usually two pairs; the fore wings being much larger than the hind wings, but the latter may be greatly reduced or even absent in some species. The fore wings are somewhat triangular in shape and the wing surface has a regular series of corrugations or fluting, with longitudinal veins lying either on a ridge or a furrow. There is little consistency in the nomenclature of the veins and several systems have been proposed. The one followed in the key is that used by Kimmins (1942, 1972) and illustrated in fig. 2.

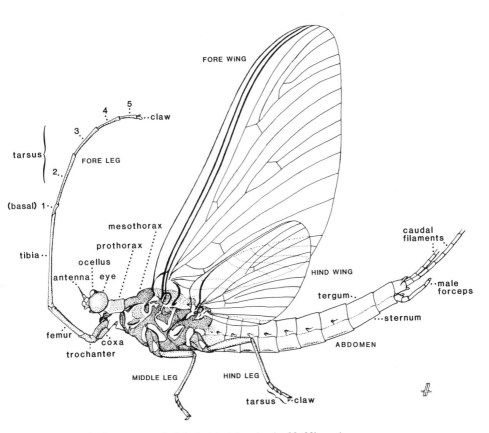

Fig. 1. Basic structure of adult (original drawing by M. Mizzaro).

The *costa* (C) forms the front edge of the fore wing, and the *subcosta* (Sc) runs parallel to it and the anterior branch of the *radius* (R_1). The posterior branch of the radius is generally separated from the anterior branch and forks to form the four veins (R_2, R_3, R_4, R_5) of the *radial sector* (R_s). A number of *intercalary veins* are present in the outer part of the radial sector, especially between R_2 and R_3. The *outer fork* (OF) is located between R_4 and R_5. The *media* or median vein has two branches (M_1, M_2), and the *cubitus* is also bifurcate with the anterior branch (Cu_1) usually longer than the posterior branch (Cu_2). There are one or more *anal veins* (A) that are usually weak and irregular. *Cross-veins* and the spaces between the major veins usually take the name of the anterior vein, e.g. the costal area and costal cross-veins are situated between the costa and subcosta. The strong cross-vein at the base of the costal and subcostal areas (i.e. the cross-vein between C and R_1) is sometimes called the *costal-brace*, or the basal, humeral or great cross-vein. The *pterostigma* is situated on the front edge of the wing towards the tip (fig. 2), and is a portion of the costal and subcostal areas. It may be heavily pigmented and have thickened and/or more numerous cross-veins.

The venation of the hind wing is often difficult or impossible to interpret, and the costa and subcosta are often more or less fused except near the base. There may be a projecting *costal process* near the base of the front edge of the hind wing.

Abdomen. There are ten segments, each of which is ring-shaped with a dorsal *tergum* (or *tergite*) and a ventral *sternum* (or *sternite*). The latter is absent in the tenth segment. The posterior part of the ninth sternum is called the *subgenital plate* (or styliger plate) in males and the *subanal plate* in females. The female oviducts are paired and open between the seventh and eighth sternites. The subgenital plate of the male gives rise to a pair of slender, and usually segmented, *forceps* (or claspers). Dorsal to the subgenital plate are the paired *penis-lobes*. These vary between species and are therefore useful taxonomic characters, except in the Baetidae in which they are membranous and extrudable.

There are two or three long *caudal filaments* (or tails) at the end of the abdomen. The outer filaments are the *cerci* and are always present in undamaged specimens. The median terminal filament is so reduced in some genera as to be effectively absent.

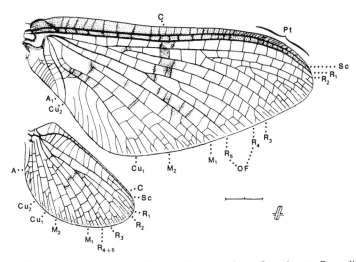

Fig. 2. Wings of *Ephemera danica*: C, costa; Pt, pterostigma; Sc, subcosta; R_1, radius; R_2, R_3, R_4, R_5, branches of radial sector (R_s); OF, outer fork; M, media; Cu, cubitus; A, anal veins. (Scale line 2 mm; original drawing by M. Mizzaro).

CLASSIFICATION AND CHECK LIST

Eaton (1883-1888) established the basis of the modern classification of Ephemeroptera but recognized only "Series" and "Sections". These were treated as families by most subsequent workers who simply added newly-discovered families (e.g. Klapálek 1909; Ulmer 1914, 1929; Schoenemund 1930). An exception was Needham (1905) who recognized only three families (see also Needham, Traver & Hsu 1935), but most workers now agree that this number is too low. There is general agreement on the composition of the families but not on the relationships between them. Several higher-classification systems have been proposed, including those by Edmunds & Traver (1954), Demoulin (1958), Chernova (1970). These systems have been reviewed by McCafferty & Edmunds (1979) who proposed two fundamental suborders for the extant families of the order.

In the suborder Schistonota (split-back mayflies), the larvae have developing forewing pads that are free for at least half of their length beyond their fusion to the thorax. There are usually well-developed gills along the abdomen and the larvae are active. In the suborder Pannota (fused-back mayflies), the forewing pads are free for less than half their length beyond their fusion to the thorax. The gills tend to be reduced and protected in various ways, and the larvae are usually sluggish until just before emergence of the subimagines. Three superfamilies and thirteen families are placed in the Schistonota, and three superfamilies and six families are placed in the Pannota (Table 1). The phylogeny of the suborders and superfamilies is illustrated in fig. 3.

Eight families occur in the British Isles, six in the Schistonota and two in the Pannota (families with asterisks in Table 1). Eighteen genera and forty-seven species are included in the check-list (Table 2). The monograph by Müller-Liebenau (1969) was used for the nomenclature in the genus *Baetis*. The species previously identified as *B. bioculatus* (L.) has been found to be *B. fuscatus*, and the true *bioculatus* belongs to another genus. *B. tenax* Eaton is now regarded as a synonym of *B. vernus*, but it may prove to be a valid species. Macan (1979) suggests that there is an ecological distinction; *tenax* is found in the upper reaches of small stony streams rising at high altitudes in the mountains of Britain whereas *vernus* is found in slow-flowing weedy rivers. *B. pumilus* (Burmeister) is now a synonym of *B. muticus*. Sowa (1975a) suggests that the name *Cloeon dipterum* covers more than one species but Macan (1979) provides reasons why the name should still be retained for British specimens. It is now

TABLE I. HIGHER CLASSIFICATION OF THE EXTANT EPHEMEROPTERA OF THE WORLD, INCLUDING SUBORDERS, SUPERFAMILIES AND FAMILIES (those with asterisks occur in the British Isles)

Suborder: SCHISTONOTA
  Superfamily: Baetoidea
    Family: Siphlonuridae*
    Family: Ametropodidae
    Family: Baetidae*
    Family: Metretopodidae
    Family: Oligoneuriidae
    Family: Heptageniidae*

  Superfamily: Leptophlebioidea
    Family: Leptophlebiidae*

  Superfamily: Ephemeroidea
    Family: Behningiidae
    Family: Potamanthidae*
    Family: Euthyplociidae
    Family: Polymitarcyidae
    Family: Ephemeridae*
    Family: Palingeniidae

Suborder: PANNOTA
  Superfamily: Ephemerelloidea
    Family: Ephemerellidae*
    Family: Tricorythidae

  Superfamily: Caenoidea
    Family: Neoephemeridae
    Family: Caenidae*

  Superfamily: Prosopistomatoidea
    Family: Baetiscidae
    Family: Prosopistomatidae

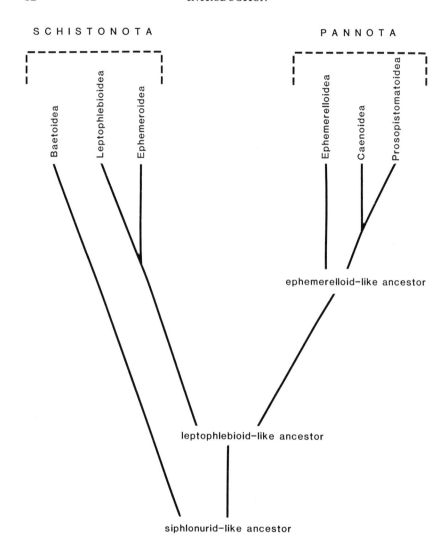

Fig. 3.   Phylogeny of the extant superfamilies and suborders of Ephemeroptera (after McCafferty & Edmunds 1979).

TABLE 2. A CHECK-LIST OF THE BRITISH EPHEMEROPTERA

Family	Genus	Species	
SIPHLONURIDAE	SIPHLONURUS Eaton, 1868	*armatus* Eaton, 1870	(1)
		lacustris Eaton, 1870	(2)
		alternatus (Say, 1824)	(3)
	AMELETUS Eaton, 1885	*inopinatus* Eaton, 1887	(4)
BAETIDAE	BAETIS Leach, 1815	*fuscatus* (Linnaeus, 1761)	(5)
		scambus Eaton, 1870	(6)
		vernus Curtis, 1834	(7)
		buceratus Eaton, 1870	(8)
		rhodani (Pictet, 1844)	(9)
		atrebatinus Eaton, 1870	(10)
		muticus (Linnaeus, 1758)	(11)
		niger (Linnaeus, 1761)	(12)
		digitatus Bengtsson, 1912	(13)
	CENTROPTILUM Eaton, 1869	*luteolum* (Müller, 1776)	(14)
		pennulatum Eaton, 1870	(15)
	CLOEON Leach, 1815	*dipterum* (Linnaeus, 1761)	(16)
		simile Eaton, 1870	(17)
	PROCLOEON Bengtsson, 1915	*bifidum* (Bengtsson, 1912)	(18)
HEPTAGENIIDAE	RHITHROGENA Eaton, 1881	*semicolorata* (Curtis, 1834)	(19)
		germanica Eaton, 1885	(20)
	HEPTAGENIA Walsh, 1863	*sulphurea* (Müller, 1776)	(21)
		longicauda (Stephens, 1835)	(22)
		fuscogrisea (Retzius, 1783)	(23)
		lateralis (Curtis, 1834)	(24)
	ARTHROPLEA Bengtsson, 1909	*congener* Bengtsson, 1909	(25)
	ECDYONURUS Eaton, 1868	*venosus* (Fabricius, 1775)	(26)
		torrentis Kimmins, 1942	(27)
		dispar (Curtis, 1834)	(28)
		insignis (Eaton, 1870)	(29)
LEPTOPHLEBIIDAE	LEPTOPHLEBIA Westwood, 1840	*marginata* (Linnaeus, 1767)	(30)
		vespertina (Linnaeus, 1758)	(31)
	PARALEPTOPHLEBIA Lestage, 1917	*submarginata* (Stephens, 1835)	(32)
		cincta (Retzius, 1783)	(33)
		werneri Ulmer, 1919	(34)
	HABROPHLEBIA Eaton, 1881	*fusca* (Curtis, 1834)	(35)
POTAMANTHIDAE	POTAMANTHUS Pictet, 1843-5	*luteus* (Linnaeus, 1767)	(36)
EPHEMERIDAE	EPHEMERA Linnaeus, 1758	*vulgata* Linnaeus, 1758	(37)
		danica Müller, 1764	(38)
		lineata Eaton, 1870	(39)
EPHEMERELLIDAE	EPHEMERELLA Walsh, 1862	*ignita* (Poda, 1761)	(40)
		notata Eaton, 1887	(41)
CAENIDAE	BRACHYCERCUS Curtis, 1834	*harrisella* Curtis, 1834	(42)
	CAENIS Stephens, 1835	*macrura* Stephens, 1835	(43)
		luctuosa (Burmeister, 1839)	(44)
		robusta Eaton, 1884	(45)
		horaria (Linnaeus, 1758)	(46)
		rivulorum Eaton, 1884	(47)

accepted that *Siphlonurus linnaeanus* (Eaton) is a synonym of *S. alternatus* (Jacob 1974a; Puthz 1977), *Procloeon pseudorufulum* Kimmins and *P. rufulum* Eaton are synonyms of *P. bifidum* (Sowa 1975b), *Rhithrogena haarupi* Esben-Petersen is a synonym of *R. germanica* (Sowa 1971), *Paraleptophlebia tumida* Bengtsson is a synonym of *P. werneri* (Landa 1969; Puthz 1978), and *Caenis moesta* Bengtsson is a synonym of *C. luctuosa* (Jacob 1974b). *Heptagenia lateralis* has not been transferred to the genus *Ecdyonurus*, as proposed by some workers (e.g. Bogoescu & Tabacaru 1962; Puthz 1978).

COLLECTION AND PRESERVATION

Adults are most readily collected with an insect net by beating bushes and trees, or sweeping low herbage near ponds, lakes, streams and rivers. A long-handled net is required for dealing with high-flying swarms. Male imagines are usually predominant in swarms whereas female imagines and subimagines of both sexes are usually found resting on vegetation during the day. *Potamanthus luteus* and some *Caenis* are active chiefly at night and are attracted to lights, whilst other *Caenis* are most active in the early morning soon after sunrise. Numerous traps have been designed to catch insects (see descriptions in Southwood 1978) and these can be used to obtain samples of adult Ephemeroptera.

Adults can be also bred from mature larvae which have characteristic black wing-pads. They are reared in a cage in a stream or in an aerated aquarium. If the emerging subimago is placed in a box with rough sides to which the insect can cling and with moistened blotting paper to maintain the humidity, then it should moult to the imago. Subimagines used for breeding should be handled carefully to avoid damage to their wings. The advantage of this method is that it yields not only an imago but also a series of larval skins and a subimago belonging to a known adult. Such a series is often useful for other taxonomic studies.

If a pinned collection is desired, adults should be brought back alive and killed with ether or chloroform. Stainless-steel pins and flat setting-boards should be used, and the specimens set in the same way as Lepidoptera, the wings, fore legs and caudal filaments being held in place by strips of paper or cellophane during drying. The male genitalia should be preserved by cutting off the apex of the abdomen and boiling it in dilute caustic potash solution (about 10%). After passing it through glacial acetic acid, it can be cleared in clove oil and then mounted in Canada balsam on a cover glass that is attached to the pin of the specimen.

It is much simpler to preserve whole specimens in fluid, e.g. 70% alcohol, dilute formaldehyde (one part of 40% formaldehyde to nineteen parts of water), or a mixture of alcohol and dilute formaldehyde. If formaldehyde is used, then the specimen should be first wetted in 70% alcohol. Another suitable fixative fluid is Pämpel's mixture (four parts of glacial acetic acid, thirty parts of distilled water, six parts of 40% formaldehyde and fifteen parts of 95% alcohol). An excellent killing fluid and preservative for material suitable for dissection is K.A.A.D. (one part of kerosene, ten parts of 95% alcohol, two parts of glacial acetic acid, one part of dioxan). All specimens should have a label written in waterproof ink, and the label should give the place of collection, preferably as a National Grid Reference, as well as the collector's name, the species name when known and the full date of collection.

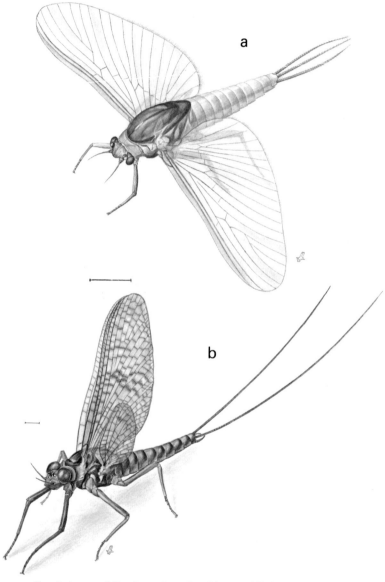

Fig. 4.   a, Female imago of *Caenis* sp.; b, male subimago of *Ecdyonurus venosus*; c, female imago of *Ephemera danica*; d, male imago of *Baetis muticus*. (Scale line 1 mm; original drawing by M. Mizzaro).

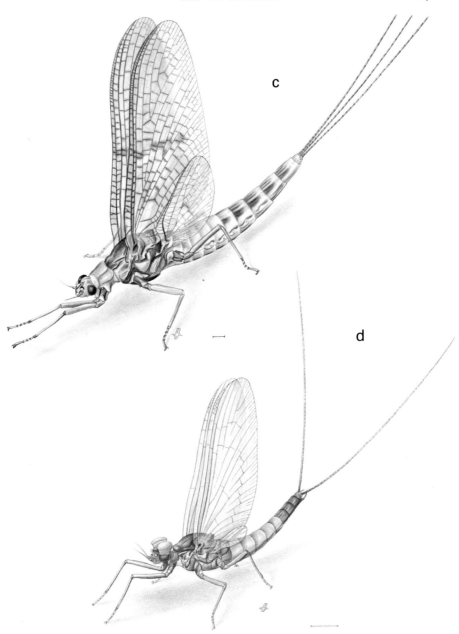

KEY TO FAMILIES

This key applies to both imagines and subimagines. Wings of imagines are not fringed with hairs, except in the Caenidae. In subimagines, the wings are fringed with minute hairs, the legs and terminal filaments are not the full length, the colours are generally duller and the male genitalia are not fully developed (fig. 4b).

1   Hind wings absent (fig. 4a)—   2

—   Hind wings present (fig. 4b, c) but may be very small (fig. 4d)—   3

2   Fore wings milky with fringed margins in both subimago and imago.   Three long caudal filaments—   CAENIDAE, p. 62

—   Fore wings hyaline (clear or transparent) and not fringed in imago.   Two long caudal filaments—   BAETIDAE, p. 29
(Genera Cloeon, Procloeon)

3(1) *Two long caudal filaments—   4

—   Three long caudal filaments—   6

4   Hind wings reduced, with only two or three major veins.   Hind tarsus with three free segments, two of the original five segments being fused to the tibia (fig. 5a)—   BAETIDAE, p. 32
(Genera Baetis, Centroptilum)

—   Hind wings not reduced and with many veins.   Hind tarsus with four or five free segments (fig. 5b, c)   5

*Where a key couplet is not reached from the preceding one, the number of the couplet from which the direction came is indicated thus in parentheses.

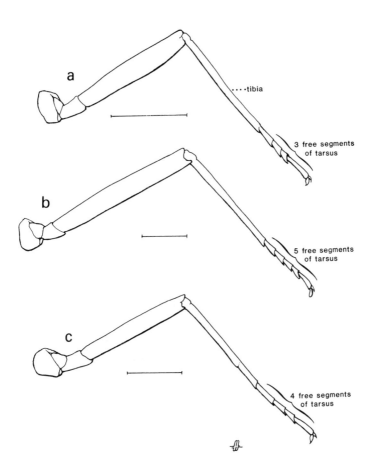

Fig. 5. Hind legs of *a*, *Baetis* (Baetidae); *b*, *Ecdyonurus* (Heptageniidae); *c*, *Siphlonurus* (Siphlonuridae). (Scale line 1 mm; original drawing by M. Mizzaro).

5   Hind tarsus with five free segments (fig. 5b). Fore wings with two pairs of cubital intercalary veins that run adjacent to Cu_1 (fig. 6a)—
HEPTAGENIIDAE, p. 38

—   Hind tarsus with four free segments, one of the original five segments being fused to the tibia (fig. 5c).   Fore wings with cubital intercalary veins that run from Cu_1 to the hind margin of the wing and form a series of veinlets that are often sinuate (fig. 6b)—
SIPHLONURIDAE, p. 24

The length and proportions of the tarsal segments may be subject to abnormalities when a leg has been damaged or lost and regenerated in the larval stage.

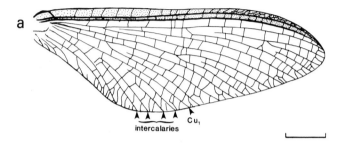

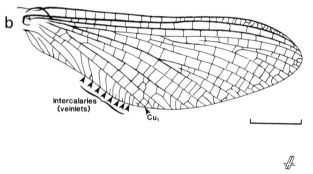

Fig. 6. Fore wings of *a, Ecdyonurus* (Heptageniidae); *b, Siphlonurus* (Siphlonuridae). (Scale line 2 mm; original drawing by M. Mizzaro).

6(3) Fore wings with M_2 and Cu_1 arched at their bases and strongly divergent from the base of M_1 (fig. 7a, b). Large (fore wing 12–24 mm long)—   7

— Fore wings with M_2 and Cu_1 not arched, and with the base of M_1 and M_2 almost parallel to the base of Cu_1 (fig. 7c, d, e). Medium-sized (fore wing <15 mm)—   8

7 Wings more or less marked with brown. A_1 in fore wing simple (fig. 7a). Abdomen light with brown markings. Eyes of males undivided—   EPHEMERIDAE, p. 58

— Wings unspotted, yellow. A_1 in fore wing forked (fig. 7b). Eyes of males divided—   POTAMANTHIDAE, p. 56

8(6) Fore wings with Cu_2 either nearer to A_1 at the base or at most midway between Cu_1 and A_1 (fig. 7c, d)—   LEPTOPHLEBIIDAE, p. 48

— Fore wings with Cu_2 nearer to Cu_1 than A_1 at the base (fig. 7e)—
                                              EPHEMERELLIDAE, p. 60

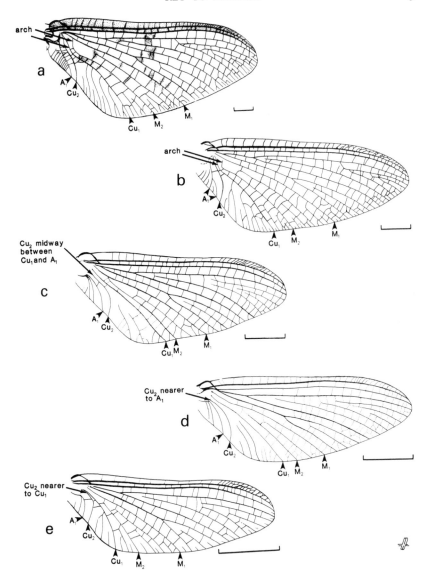

Fig. 7. Fore wings of *a*, *Ephemera* (Ephemeridae); *b*, *Potamanthus* (Potamanthidae); *c*, *Leptophlebia* (Leptophlebiidae); *d*, *Paraleptophlebia* (Leptophlebiidae); *e*, *Ephemerella* (Ephemerellidae). (Scale line 2 mm; original drawing by M. Mizzaro).

KEY TO SPECIES

Family SIPHLONURIDAE

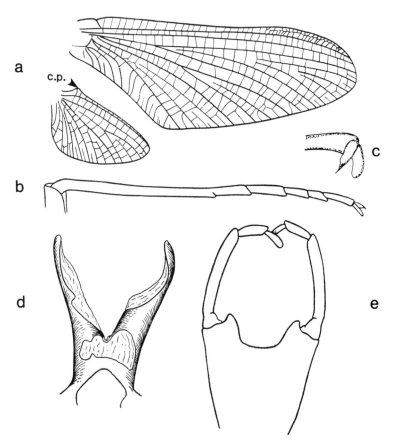

Fig. 8. *Ameletus inopinatus*: *a*, wings (c.p. = costal process in hind wing); *b*, hind tibia and tarsus; *c*, tarsal claws; *d*, penis lobes (dorsal); *e*, forceps (ventral).

1   Hind tarsus is slightly shorter than the tibia (fig. 8*b*); claws are dissimi-
    lar (one sharp, one blunt) (fig. 8*c*); costal process of hind wing is acute
    (fig. 8*a*); wings are dark brown in imago and reddish or yellowish
    brown in subimago; penis-lobes of male are slender with a deep
    median excision (fig. 8*d, e*)—   **Ameletus inopinatus** Eaton

Flight period May–August.   Larvae found chiefly in mountain streams but also
recorded from several lochs in northwest Scotland.

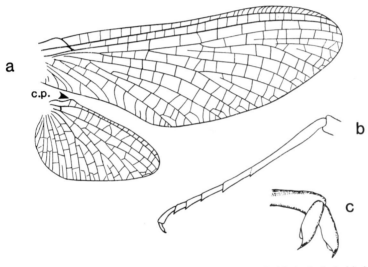

Fig. 9.   *Siphlonurus lacustris*: *a*, wings (c.p. = costal process in hind wing); *b*, hind tibia
and tarsus; *c*, tarsal claws.

—   Hind tarsus is slightly longer than the tibia (fig. 9*b*); both claws are
    sharp (fig. 9*c*); costal process of hind wing is obtuse or weak (fig. 9*a*);
    other characters not as above—   **2**

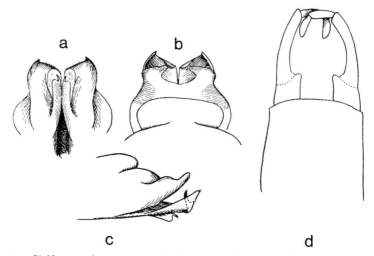

Fig. 10. *Siphlonurus alternatus*: *a*, penis lobes (ventral); *b*, penis lobes (dorsal); *c*, penis
lobes (lateral); *d*, forceps (ventral).

2   Femora have a dark reddish brown transverse band on the outer
surface before the junction with the tibia; penis-lobes of male imagines
are fairly blunt (fig. 10); wings of subimagines are greyish with a
distinct pale border on the outer margin of the hind wings—

Siphlonurus alternatus (Say)

Flight period May–August.   Larvae found chiefly in calcareous lakes and deep
pools in slow-flowing rivers.

—   Femora are unbanded; penis-lobes of male imagines are elongate (figs
11, 12); hind wings of subimagines without pale border—   **3**

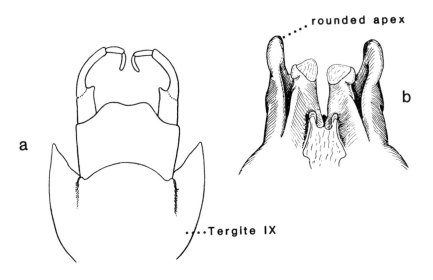

rounded apex

b

a

Tergite IX

Fig. 11. *Siphlonurus armatus*: *a*, forceps (ventral); *b*, penis lobes (dorsal).

3 Tergite IX is clearly widened with strongly pointed hind angles; penis-lobes of male imagines are elongate and rounded at apices (fig. 11); wings of subimagines are brownish grey with cross-veins clearly visible— **Siphlonurus armatus** Eaton

Flight period May–August. Larvae found chiefly in lakes, ponds and slow-flowing streams and rivers.

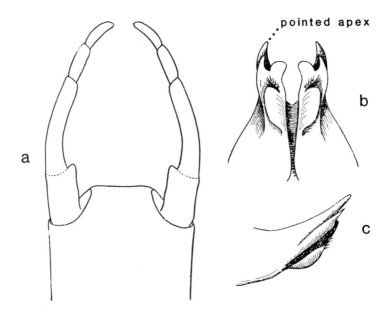

pointed apex

a

b

c

Fig. 12.　*Siphlonurus lacustris*: *a*, forceps (ventral); *b*, penis lobes (ventral); *c*, penis lobes (lateral).

— Tergite IX has only slightly produced hind angles; penis-lobes of male imagines are elongate and pointed at apices (fig. 12); wings of subimagines are greenish grey with dark main veins and indistinct cross-veins—　　　　　　　　**Siphlonurus lacustris** Eaton

Flight period May–September.　Larvae found chiefly in lakes, slow-flowing sections of streams and rivers, and ponds at high altitudes.

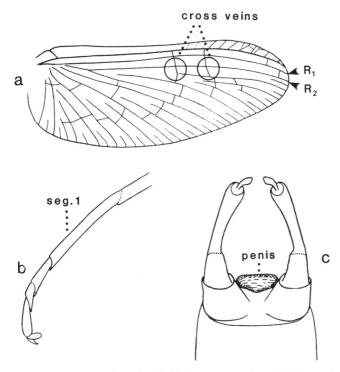

Fig. 13. *Procloeon bifidum*: *a*, fore wing; *b*, hind tarsus; *c*, male genitalia (ventral).

Family BAETIDAE

1 Hind wings absent—   2

— Hind wings present but reduced, with only two or three major veins—

                                                                   4

2 First segment of hind tarsus is about three times the length of the second (fig. 13*b*); two major cross-veins between R_1 and R_2 are in line with cross-veins below them (fig. 13*a*); penis of male imago appears flat in ventral view (fig. 13*c*)—   **Procloeon bifidum** (Bengtsson)

Flight period April–October.   Larvae found chiefly in slow-flowing sections of streams and rivers.

—   First segment of hind tarsus is about twice the length of the second
    (fig. 14b); two major cross-veins between R_1 and R_2 are not in line
    with cross-veins below them (fig. 14a); penis of male imago appears
    either triangular or trapezoidal in ventral view (fig. 14c, e)—   **3**

3   Pterostigma has three to five cross-veins (fig. 14a); forceps of male
    imago are slender and penis appears triangular in ventral view (fig.
    14c); costal and subcostal areas of fore wing in female imago are
    yellowish brown—   **Cloeon dipterum** (Linnaeus)

Flight period May–October.   Larvae found chiefly in small productive ponds,
shallow water in lakes and slow-flowing sections of streams and rivers.

—   Pterostigma has nine to eleven cross-veins (fig. 14d); forceps of male
    imago are stout and penis appears trapezoidal in ventral view (fig.
    14e); costal and subcostal areas of fore wings in female imago are not
    coloured—   **Cloeon simile** Eaton

Flight period March–November.   Larvae found chiefly in small ponds, slow-
flowing sections of streams and rivers, and also amongst vegetation in the deeper
water of ponds and lakes.

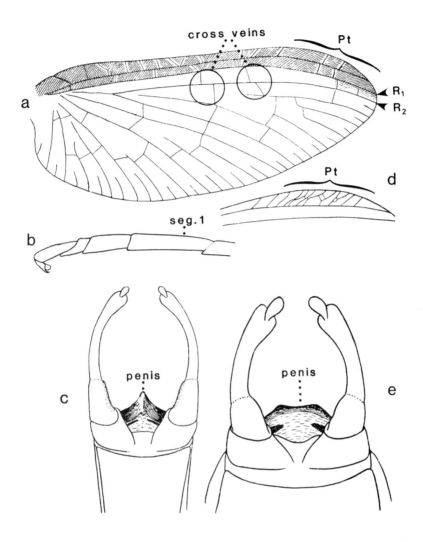

Fig. 14. *Cloeon dipterum*: *a*, fore wing (Pt = pterostigma); *b*, hind tarsus; *c*, male genitalia (ventral)
Cloeon simile: *d*, pterostigmatic region of fore wing (Pt = pterostigma); *e*, male genitalia (ventral).

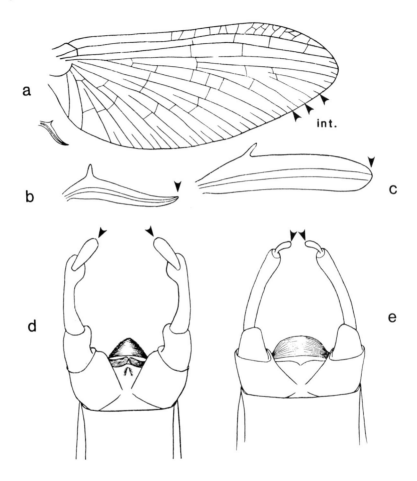

Fig. 15. *Centroptilum* spp.: *a*, wings (int. = intercalary veins); *b*, hind wing of *C. luteolum*; *c*, hind wing of *C. pennulatum*; *d*, male genitalia (ventral) of *C. luteolum*; *e*, male genitalia (ventral) of *C. pennulatum*.

4(1) Single intercalary veins along outer margin of fore wing (fig. 15*a*)—

                                                                           5

—   Paired intercalary veins along outer margin of fore wing (fig. 16)— **6**

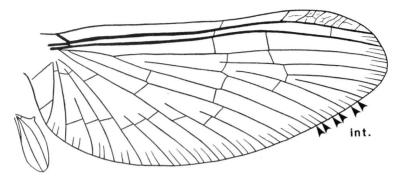

Fig. 16. *Baetis*: wings (int. = intercalary veins).

5 Apex of hind wing is pointed (fig. 15*b*); abdominal segments II-VII of male imago are translucent–whitish; terminal segments of forceps of male imago are large (fig. 15*d*); small species (length of fore wing 6–7 mm)— **Centroptilum luteolum** (Müller)

Flight period April–November. Larvae found chiefly on stony shores of lakes and in slow-flowing sections of streams and rivers, especially amongst vegetation and on sandy bottoms.

— Apex of hind wing is round (fig. 15*c*); abdominal segments II-VI of male imago are translucent–whitish and apical margins are reddish orange; terminal segments of forceps of male imago are small (fig. 15*e*); large species (length of fore wing 9 mm)— **Centroptilum pennulatum** Eaton

Flight period May–October. Larvae found chiefly in slow-flowing sections of streams and rivers, especially amongst vegetation and on sandy bottoms.

6(4) Costal process absent (fig. 17*a*); a small pointed toothlike process present between the bases of the forceps of the male imago— **Baetis atrebatinus** Eaton

Flight period May–October. Larvae found chiefly in calcareous streams and rivers.

— Costal process present near base of hind wing (e.g. fig. 17*b*, *d*, *e*); no toothlike process present between male forceps— 7

7   Hind wing has two longitudinal veins, the second of which is forked
(fig. 17*b*)—   8

—   Hind wing has three longitudinal veins (fig. 17*d*, *e*)—   9

8   Forceps in male imago have no marked constriction at the junction of
the second and third segments, and the fourth segment is only about
half the length of the third segment (fig. 17*b*)—
Baetis niger (Linnaeus)

Flight period April–October.   Larvae found chiefly amongst vegetation in streams
and rivers.

—   Forceps in male imago have a marked constriction at the junction of
the second and third segments, and the fourth segment is about two-
thirds the length of the third segment (fig. 17*c*)—
Baetis digitatus Bengtsson

Flight period May–September.   Larvae found chiefly amongst vegetation in
streams and rivers.

(Subimagines and female imagines of these two species cannot be separated at
present.)

9(7) Second longitudinal vein in hind wing is forked (fig. 17*d*); forceps in
male imago have a very short fourth segment that is almost spherical—
Baetis muticus (Linnaeus)

Flight period April–October.   Larvae found chiefly in small stony streams and
rivers.

—   Second longitudinal vein in hind wing is not forked (e.g. fig. 17*e*)—
10

This vein is occasionally forked in *B. buceratus* but the forceps of male
imagines of the latter species are strongly arched, unlike those of *B. muticus* —
cf. figs 17*d* and 18*d*, *e*.

NOTE: the following key to the remaining five *Baetis* species is applicable
only to male imagines, except for subimagines of *B. rhodani* with their
characteristic markings (fig. 18*f*).

10   Second segment of the forceps has a small toothlike process on its
inner margin (fig. 17*e*)—   **Baetis vernus** Curtis

Flight period April–October.   Larvae found chiefly in slow-flowing sections of
rivers and in the upper reaches of small stony streams rising at high altitudes.

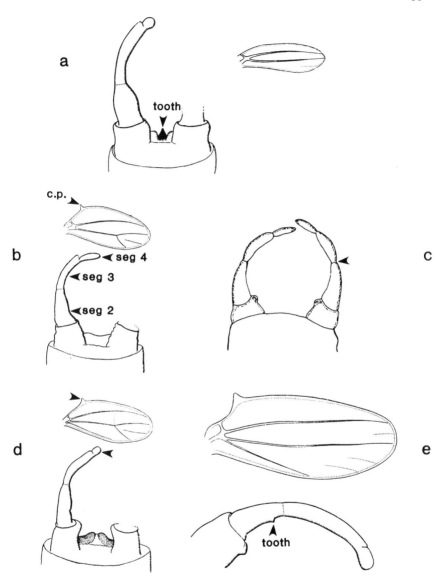

Fig. 17. *Baetis* spp.: *a*, hind wing and male genitalia (ventral) of *B. atrebatinus*; *b*, hind wing (c.p. = costal process) and male genitalia (ventral) of *B. niger*; *c*, male genitalia (ventral) of *B. digitatus*; *d*, hind wing and male genitalia (ventral) of *B. muticus*; *e*, hind wing and male forcep (ventral) of *B. vernus*.

— Second segment of the forceps has no toothlike process—   11

11 Basal segment of forceps has a small toothlike process at the inner distal corner (fig. 18*a*, *b*)—   12

— Basal segment of forceps has no toothlike process but is more extensively swollen (fig. 18*c*, *d*)—   13

12 Turbinate eyes (upper part of eye turret-shaped) are lemon yellow; third segment of forceps is slightly swollen so that there is a marked constriction at the junction of the second and third segments (fig. 18*a*)—   **Baetis fuscatus** (Linnaeus)

Flight period May–October. Larvae found chiefly amongst vegetation and on sand and gravel in rivers, possibly with a preference for calcareous waters.

— Turbinate eyes are sepia brown; forceps are slender with only a slight constriction at the junction of the second and third segments (fig. 18*b*)—   **Baetis scambus** Eaton

Flight period February–November. Larvae found chiefly amongst vegetation and on sand and gravel in streams and rivers.

13(11) Basal segment of forceps has a large swelling distally on the inner margin (fig. 18*d*); forceps are arched in lateral view so that distal part points downwards towards the ventral surface (fig. 18*e*)—   **Baetis buceratus** Eaton

Flight period April–October. Larvae found chiefly in rivers.

— Basal segment of forceps has only a slight swelling distally on the inner margin (fig. 18*c*); forceps are not arched in lateral view; metatergum (dorsal surface of posterior segment of thorax) of subimago is marked with two open circles that are unique to this species (fig. 18*f*)—   **Baetis rhodani** (Pictet)

Flight period usually March–November but adults have been taken in all months. Larvae found in streams and rivers; this is the commonest species in this genus.

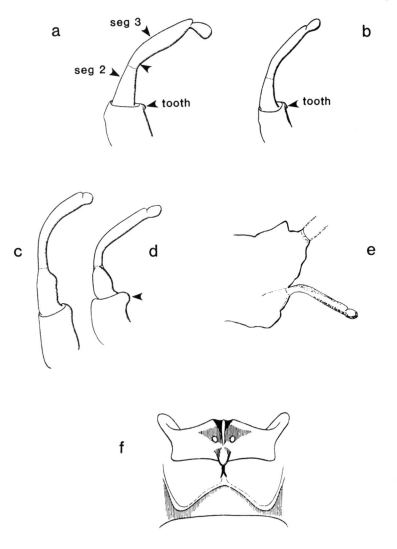

Fig. 18. *Baetis* spp.: *a*, male forcep (ventral) of *B. fuscatus*; *b*, male forcep (ventral) of *B. scambus*; *c*, male forcep (ventral) of *B. rhodani*; *d*, male forcep (ventral) of *B. buceratus*; *e*, male forcep (lateral) of *B. buceratus*; *f*, metatergum of subimago of *B. rhodani*.

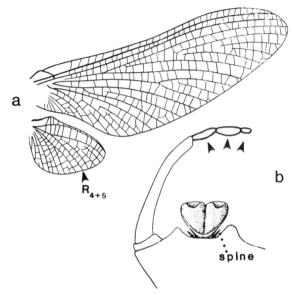

Fig. 19. *Arthroplea congener*: *a*, wings; *b*, male genitalia (ventral with one forcep omitted).

Family HEPTAGENIIDAE

1   Vein R_{4+5} in hind wing is simple and unforked (fig. 19*a*); segments
one to four of male fore tarsus are of similar length and about twice
the length of the fifth terminal segment; penis-lobes of male imagines
have a long spine on each side at the base and the male forceps have
three short terminal segments (fig. 19*b*)—

Arthroplea congener Bengtsson

Flight period May–June.   Larvae found chiefly in slow-flowing water (this species
may no longer occur in the British Isles).

—   Vein R_{4+5} in hind wing is forked (figs 20*a*, 21*a*, 24*a*); segment one of
male fore tarsus is shorter than one or more of the other four tarsal
segments (e.g. figs 24*b*, 25*a*); penis-lobes of male imagines do not
have long spines at their base and the male forceps have two short
terminal segments (e.g. fig. 20*c*, *d*)—   2

2   A dark mark occurs near the centre of each femur (fig. 20*b*); penis-
lobes of male imagines are cylindrical and widely separated by a U-
shaped excision in the forceps-base (fig. 20*c*, *d*)—   3

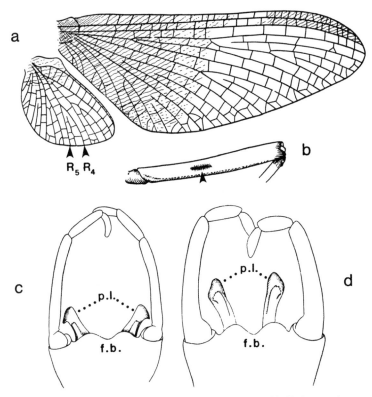

Fig. 20. *Rhithrogena* spp.: *a*, wings of *R. semicolorata*; *b*, femur with distinct mark; *c*, male genitalia (ventral) of *R. semicolorata* (p.l. = penis-lobe; f.b. = forceps-base); *d*, male genitalia (ventral) of *R. germanica*.

— No dark mark near centre of each femur; penis-lobes of male imagines are contiguous and not cylindrical (figs 23, 24*d*, *e*, 25*c*, *d*)—   4

3 Small species (length of fore wing 9–13 mm); wings of subimagines are pale mouse-grey with no black borders to the cross-veins; wings of imagines are tinted pale golden brown in their basal half (fig. 20*a*); penis-lobes of male imagines are truncate and terminate obliquely with a distinct hook-like projection facing outwards (fig. 20*c*)—
Rhithrogena semicolorata (Curtis)

Flight period April–September.   Larvae found chiefly in stony streams and rivers.

— Large species (length of fore wing 12–17 mm); wings of subimagines are pale yellowish grey with black borders to the cross-veins; wings of imagines are indistinctly brownish at base; penis-lobes of male imagines are truncate and terminate obliquely with no outward projection (fig. 20*d*)— **Rhithrogena germanica** Eaton

Flight period late March–early May.   Larvae found chiefly in large, fast-flowing rivers.

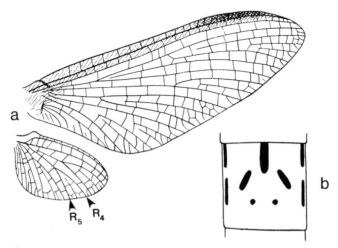

Fig. 21.   *Ecdyonurus* spp.: *a*, wings of *E. venosus*; *b*, markings on abdominal sternite of *E. insignis*.

4(2) Penis-lobes spread outwards distally to form a broad T-shape (fig. 23*a, b, c, d*)—   **5**

— Penis-lobes do not form T-shape but either have a blunt projection distally (figs 24*d, e*, 25*d*) or are rounded (fig. 25*c*)—   **8**

5 Abdominal sternites of both subimagines and imagines are marked with three black lines and two black spots on a yellow background (fig. 21*b*)— **Ecdyonurus insignis** (Eaton)

Flight period May–October.   Larvae found chiefly in stony rivers.

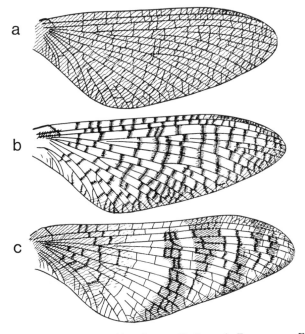

Fig. 22. Fore wings of *Ecdyonurus* subimagines: *a*, *E. dispar*; *b*, *E. venosus*; *c*, *E. torrentis*.

— Sternites are not marked as above and background colour is reddish
  brown—   **6**

6 Fore wings of subimagines are mottled, with black borders to all
   cross-veins (fig. 22*b*); forceps-base in male imagines is dome-shaped
   with no teeth or projections (fig. 23*b*); ratio of male fore tibia to tarsus
   is 1:1.5—   **Ecdyonurus venosus** (Fabricius)

Flight period April–October.   Larvae found chiefly in stony rivers and streams.

— Fore wings of subimagines are not mottled or are mottled unevenly
  in blackish bands (fig. 22*a*, *c*); forceps-base in male imagines has teeth
  or projections (fig. 23*c*, *d*); ratio of male fore tibia to tarsus is about
  1:1.9—   **7**

7   Fore wings of subimagines are uniformly greyish yellow and the cross-veins do not have strongly black borders (fig. 22*a*); forceps-base in male imagines has two pointed teeth that curve inwards (fig. 23*c*)—
Ecdyonurus dispar (Curtis)

Flight period June–October.   Larvae found chiefly in stony rivers and on lake shores.

—   Fore wings of subimagines are mottled, with black borders to some cross-veins, so that there are transverse blackish bands across the wing (fig. 22*c*); forceps-base in male imagines has two blunt teeth that do not curve inwards (fig. 23*d*)—   **Ecdyonurus torrentis** Kimmins

Flight period March–September.   Larvae found chiefly in stony streams and rivers.

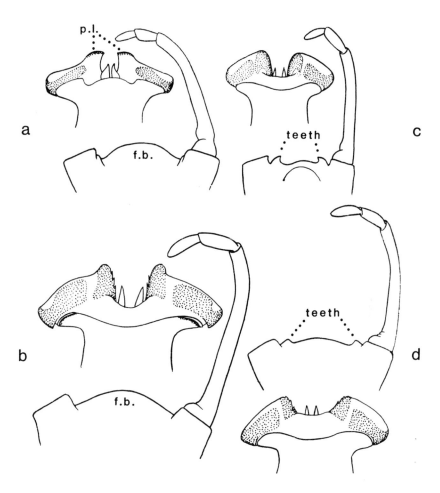

Fig. 23. Male genitalia of *Ecdyonurus* spp.: f.b. = forceps base with right forcep, p.l. = penis lobes (dorsal and more enlarged than forceps base); *a*, *E. insignis*; *b*, *E. venosus*; *c*, *E. dispar*; *d*, *E. torrentis*.

8(4) Fore wings of subimagines are yellow or greenish yellow; basal segment (seg. 1) of hind tarsus is shorter than the second segment (fig. 24c); forceps-base of male imagines has no toothlike projections (fig. 24d, e)—   **9**

— Fore wings of subimagines are grey or greyish yellow; basal segment (seg. 1) of hind tarsus is equal to or longer than the second segment (fig. 25b); forceps-base of male imagines has two blunt toothlike projections (fig. 25c, d)—   **10**

9 Anterior femora have two flesh-coloured rings, one midway, one at distal end; side of metathorax has a small black spot above the coxa of the hind leg; general colour is yellowish brown and abdominal segments II-VIII in the male imago are translucent; wings are coloured pale yellow but the colour is stronger in costal and subcostal areas—
Heptagenia longicauda (Stephens)

Flight period late May–June.   Larvae found chiefly in large rivers (this species may no longer occur in the British Isles).

— Anterior femora are not marked as above; side of thorax has a short black line just behind the coxa of the fore leg and one to three black dots above the coxa of the middle leg; general colour is light yellowish brown in male imagines and yellow in female imagines; the predominant colour of both body and wings is a bright sulphureous yellow (hence the species name)—   **Heptagenia sulphurea** (Müller)

Flight period early May–October.   Larvae found chiefly in lower reaches of rivers and in calcareous lakes.

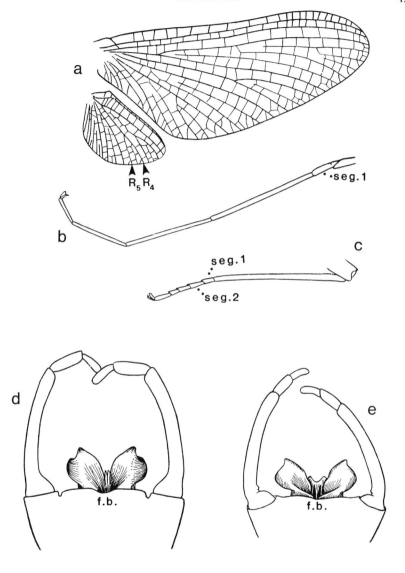

Fig. 24. *Heptagenia sulphurea*: *a*, wings; *b*, male fore tarsus; *c*, male hind tibia and tarsus; *d*, male genitalia (ventral). *H. longicauda*: *e*, male genitalia (f.b. = forceps base).

10(8) Fore wings of subimagines are grey and may be marked faintly with transverse bands; both subimagines and imagines have no reddish brown bands on the femora of their legs; thorax of imago has a bright yellow streak running from the base of the fore wing towards the head; penis-lobes of male imagines are rounded distally (fig. 25c)—
Heptagenia lateralis (Curtis)

Flight period May–September.   Larvae found chiefly in stony streams and rivers, and on stony shores of lakes.

—   Fore wings of subimagines are greyish yellow with darker veins and cross-veins; both subimagines and imagines have two reddish brown bands on each femur; thorax of imago has no bright yellow streak; penis-lobes of male imagines have a blunt projection distally and an excision on the outer margin (fig. 25d)—
Heptagenia fuscogrisea (Retzius)

Flight period May–June.   Larvae found chiefly on the stony substratum of calcareous rivers and lakes, especially in Ireland.

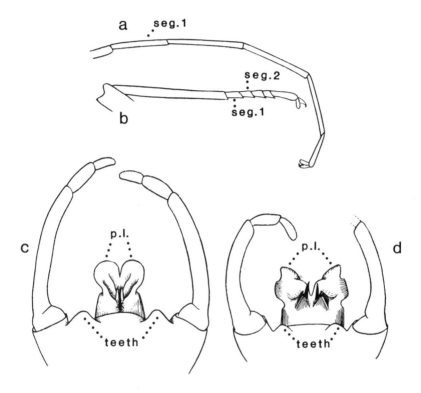

Fig. 25. *Heptagenia lateralis*: *a*, male fore tarsus; *b*, male hind tibia and tarsus; *c*, male genitalia (ventral). *H. fuscogrisea*: *d*, male genitalia (ventral) (p.l. = penis lobes).

Family LEPTOPHLEBIIDAE

1   Hind wing has a costal process about half way along the costal margin
     and a very broad costal area near its base (fig. 26*a*, *b*); segments 2 and
     3 of forceps each about half the length of segment 1 in male imagines
     (fig. 26*c*, *d*)—   **Habrophlebia fusca** (Curtis)

Flight period May–September.   Larvae found chiefly in slow-flowing streams with
aquatic macrophytes or dead leaves, sometimes in rivers.

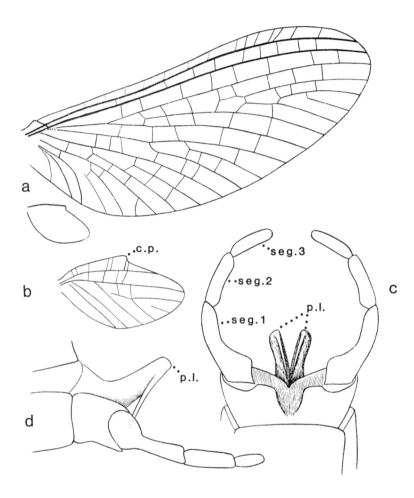

Fig. 26. *Habrophlebia fusca*: *a*, wings; *b*, hind wing (c.p. = costal process); *c*, male genitalia (ventral); *d*, male genitalia (lateral) (p.l. = penis lobes).

— Hind wing has no costal process and costal area is long and narrow
    (figs 27a, 28a, b); segments 2 and 3 of forceps much smaller than half
    the length of segment 1 in male imagines (figs 27b, c, 29)—   2

2   Base of vein Cu_2 in fore wing lies about mid-way between veins Cu_1
    and A_1 (fig. 27a)—   3

—   Base of vein Cu_2 in fore wing lies closer to vein A_1 than to vein Cu_1
    (fig. 28a, b)—   4

3   Fore wings of subimagines are brownish grey in fresh specimens,
    the cross-veins have brownish margins and the hind wings are not
    obviously paler than the fore wings; fore wings of imagines are brown-
    ish, especially around the pterostigma (fig. 27a) and the veins are
    brownish yellow; penis-lobes of male imagines are rounded at apices
    and each has a long recurved finger-like process (fig. 27b)—
                                    Leptophlebia marginata (Linnaeus)

Flight period April–June.   Larvae found chiefly in ponds, lakes and slow-flowing
streams.

—   Fore wings of subimagines are pale grey in fresh specimens, the cross-
    veins are not margined and the hind wings are obviously paler than
    the fore wings; fore wings of imagines are clear and colourless except
    for brownish veins C, Sc and R_1; penis-lobes of male imagines have
    hook-like apices and each has a recurved blade-like process (fig. 27c)—
                                    Leptophlebia vespertina (Linnaeus)

Flight period April–August.   Larvae found chiefly in ponds, lakes and slow-
flowing streams.

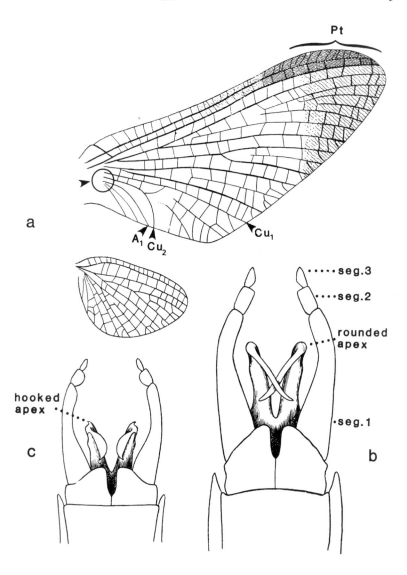

Fig. 27. *Leptophlebia* spp.: *a*, wings of *L. marginata* (Pt = pterostigma); *b*, male genitalia (ventral) of *L. marginata*; *c*, male genitalia (ventral) of *L. vespertina*.

4(2) Largest species in genus (length of fore wing 10–13 mm); wings of
     subimagines have heavily shaded cross-veins and a distinctly pale area
     in the centre of the fore wing (fig. 28*b*), but this pattern is absent in
     the clearer wings of the imagines (fig. 28*a*); penis-lobes of male ima-
     gines are only slightly divided by a small excision at their apex, and
     each lobe carries two long, pointed processes at its apex, one process
     directed outwards and the other downwards (fig. 29*a*, *b*)—
                              Paraleptophlebia submarginata (Stephens)

Flight period April–July.   Larvae found chiefly in stony streams and rivers.

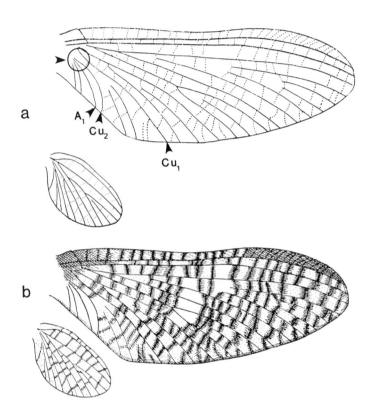

Fig. 28. *Paraleptophlebia submarginata*, male: *a*, wings of imago; *b*, wings of subimago.

— Smaller species (length of fore wing 5–9 mm); wings of subimagines
   are uniformly grey and not marked as above; penis-lobes of male
   imagines are clearly divided by a deep excision (fig. 29c, d, e, f);
   processes on penis-lobes are not as above—   5

5 Wings of subimagines are blackish grey and those of imagines are
   generally clear; abdominal segments II-VII of male are translucent
   and white; tail filaments are white in male and yellow in female; penis-
   lobes of male imagines are rounded at their apices which are divided
   by a deep U-shaped excision and each carries a short blunt process
   and a long pointed process (fig. 29c, d)—

                              Paraleptophlebia cincta (Retzius)

Flight period May–August.   Larvae found chiefly in streams and rivers.

— Wings of subimagines are pale grey and those of imagines are smoky
   brown; abdominal segments III-VI of male are translucent and pale
   brown; tail filaments are greyish brown; penis-lobes of male imagines
   have widely diverging apices which are separated by a very deep
   excision, and two long, pointed processes arise from about the middle
   of the ventral surface of each penis-lobe (fig. 29e, f); the long basal
   segment of the forceps is swollen about half-way along its length,
   unlike that of the preceding species (cf. fig. 29c, e)—

                              Paraleptophlebia werneri Ulmer

Flight period May–June.   Larvae found chiefly in calcareous streams abundant
in vegetation and also in streams that cease to flow in summer.

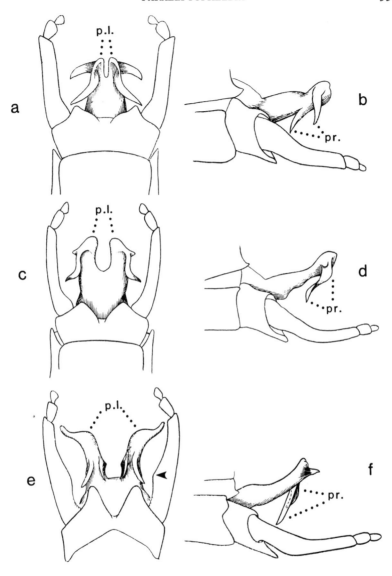

Fig. 29. *Paraleptophlebia* spp., male genitalia; ventral (*a, c, e*) and lateral (*b, d, f*): *a, b, P. submarginata*; *c, d, P. cincta*; *e, f, P. werneri*; (p.l. = penis lobes, pr. = process).

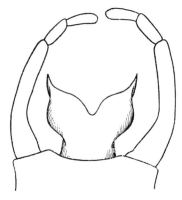

Fig. 30. *Potamanthus luteus*: male genitalia (ventral).

Family POTAMANTHIDAE

Only one species occurs in the British Isles. Wings are yellowish in
subimagines with greenish grey patches in female subimagines, and
are pale yellow in imagines with a brighter yellow costal area of the
fore wing; general colour of abdomen in subimagines and imagines is
yellow with a broad longitudinal brown stripe on the dorsal surface;
abdominal tergites II-IX have a black dot laterally at the base; male
genitalia have a characteristic shape (fig. 30)—

Potamanthus luteus (Linnaeus)

Flight period May–July. Larvae found chiefly in large rivers, often in side pools
with a bottom of stones and sand.

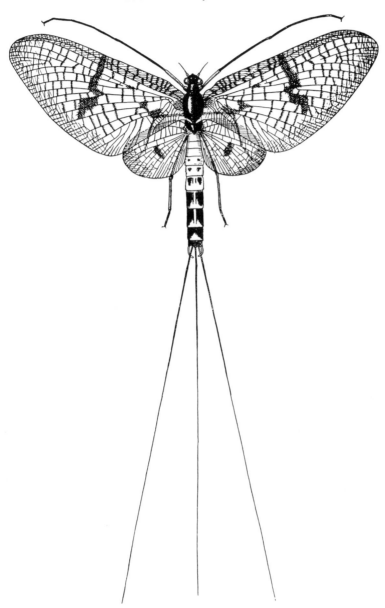

Fig. 31. *Ephemera danica*: male imago.

Family EPHEMERIDAE

1   Dorsal surface of abdomen in subimagines and imagines has characteristic markings (figs 31, 32*b*), but tergites I-V may have no markings
in some specimens, especially females; general colour of abdomen is
greyish white and wings of imagines have large, dark olive-brown
markings (fig. 31); combined length of segments 3 and 4 of male
forceps is more than half the length of segment 2 (fig. 32*e*)—
Ephemera danica Müller

Flight period April–November.   Larvae found chiefly in lakes and fast-flowing
streams and rivers with a sandy or gravelly bottom.

—   Abdominal markings are not as above (fig. 32*a*, *c*); general colour of
abdomen is yellowish to reddish brown and wings of imagines do not
have large dark olive-brown spots; combined length of segments 3
and 4 of male forceps is less than half the length of segment 2 (fig.
32*d*, *f*)—   2

2   Dorsal surface of abdomen in subimagines and imagines has characteristic markings with six longitudinal stripes on tergites V-IX or VI-IX
(fig. 32*c*); wings of imagines are pale yellowish brown with small
brown spots—   **Ephemera lineata** Eaton

Flight period July.   Larvae found chiefly in large rivers.

—   Dorsal surface of abdomen in subimagines and imagines has characteristic markings with two dark brown triangles on each tergite and a
pair of longitudinal stripes in the middle of tergites V-IX or VI-IX
(fig. 32*a*); wings of imagines are pale warm brown with reddish brown
spots—   **Ephemera vulgata** Linnaeus

Flight period May–August.   Larvae found chiefly in rivers with a muddy bottom.

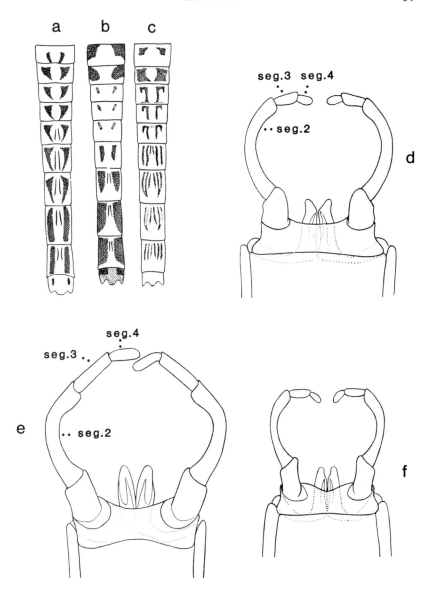

Fig. 32. *Ephemera* spp., pattern on dorsal surface of abdomen (*a*, *b*, *c*), male genitalia, ventral (*d*, *e*, *f*): *a*, *d*, *E. vulgata*; *b*, *e*, *E. danica*; *c*, *f*, *E. lineata*.

Family EPHEMERELLIDAE

1   Ventral surface of abdomen in subimagines and imagines has characteristic markings with two diagonal stripes, two lateral stripes and two central dots on sternites I-VII or I-VIII (fig. 33*a*, *b*); wings and body are yellowish brown or yellow, especially in females; penis-lobes of male imagines are separated by a deep V-shaped excision (fig. 33*c*)—
Ephemerella notata (Eaton)

Flight period May–June.   Larvae found chiefly in moderately fast-flowing rivers.

—   Ventral surface of abdomen does not have markings as above; wings and body of imagines are reddish brown, especially in females; body of subimagines is olive brown in male and green in female; penis-lobes of male imagines are separated by a small U-shaped excision (fig. 33*d*)—   **Ephemerella ignita** (Poda)

Flight period April–September.   Larvae found in fast-flowing streams and rivers, especially where aquatic vegetation is present.

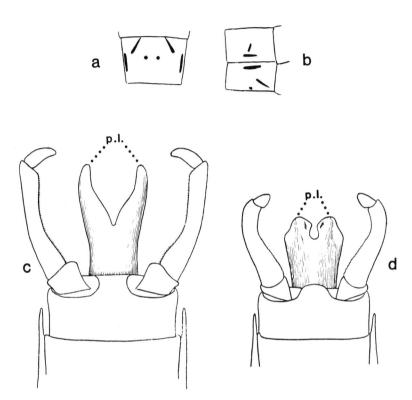

Fig. 33. *Ephemerella* spp.: *E. notata*; pattern on *a*, ventral surface, *b*, lateral surface of abdomen; *c*, male genitalia of *E. notata*; *d*, male genitalia of *E. ignita* (p.l. = penis lobes).

Family CAENIDAE

1   Prosternum (ventral portion of first segment of thorax) has a broad
    inter-coxal process, so that coxae of fore legs are wide apart (fig. 34*a*);
    second segment of antenna is elongate and about three times the length
    of the first segment (fig. 34*a*); genitalia of male imagines are as shown
    in fig. 34*c*—   **Brachycercus harrisella** Curtis

Flight period July, possibly longer.   Larvae found chiefly in rivers and especially
in mud and silt.

—   Prosternum has a very narrow inter-coxal process so that coxae of fore
    legs are close together (fig. 34*b*); second segment of antenna is short
    and about twice the length of the first segment (fig. 34*b*); genitalia of
    male imagines are as shown in fig. 35—   2

2   Dorsal surface of abdomen has a small median spine on the posterior
    margin of the second tergite (the spine is often easier to see in lateral
    view but may not be obvious in subimagines and dried specimens in
    a pinned collection); tail filaments are white or yellowish-white—   3

—   Dorsal surface of abdomen does not have median spine as above; tail
    filaments are brownish grey or greyish white and may have darker
    rings at regular intervals—   5

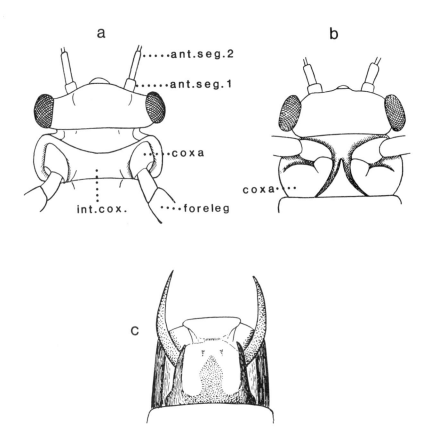

Fig. 34. *Brachycercus* and *Caenis* spp.: *a*, head and prothorax of *B. harrisella* (ventral); *b*, head and prothorax of *Caenis* (ventral); *c*, male genitalia of *B. harrisella* (ventral) (ant. seg. = antennal segment, int. cox. = inter-coxal process).

3   Smallest of the British Ephemeroptera (length of fore wing 2-3 mm); dorsal surface of abdomen has greyish markings on tergites I-III only; penis-lobes of male imagines are divided by a V-shaped excision (fig. 35*a*, but note that the excision is usually not as deep as that shown on the figure)—   **Caenis rivulorum** Eaton

Flight period May–September.   Larvae found chiefly in stony streams and rivers.

—   Larger species (length of fore wing 4-6 mm); dorsal surface of abdomen has greyish markings on all tergites or on tergites I-V or I-VI; penis-lobes of male imagines are truncate and undivided (fig. 35*b*, *c*)—   **4**

4   Dorsal surface of abdomen has greyish markings on all tergites; forceps of male imagines are small and much shorter than penis-lobes (fig. 35*b*)—   **Caenis robusta** Eaton

Flight period late June–July.   Larvae found chiefly in ponds, rivers and canals, and especially in mud that is rich in organic matter.

—   Dorsal surface of abdomen has greyish markings on tergites I-V or I-VI; forceps of male imagines are long and extend beyond the penis-lobes (fig. 35*c*)—   **Caenis horaria** (Linnaeus)

Flight period May–September.   Larvae found chiefly in large rivers, canals and lakes, and especially in mud and silt.

5(2)   Base of terminal bristle on antenna is dilated (fig. 35*d*); penis-lobes of male imagines are divided by a broad excision (fig. 35*f*); pigmented area on forceps base is flask-shaped (fig. 35*f*)—   **Caenis luctuosa** (Burmeister)

Flight period June–September.   Larvae found chiefly in rivers, lakes and ponds, and especially amongst silt trapped between gravel and stones.

—   Base of terminal bristle on antenna is not dilated (fig. 35*e*); penis-lobes of male imagines are truncate and not divided (fig. 35*g*); pigmented area on forceps-base is oval (fig. 35*g*)—   **Caenis macrura** Stephens

Flight period May–August.   Larvae found chiefly in rivers and especially amongst silt.

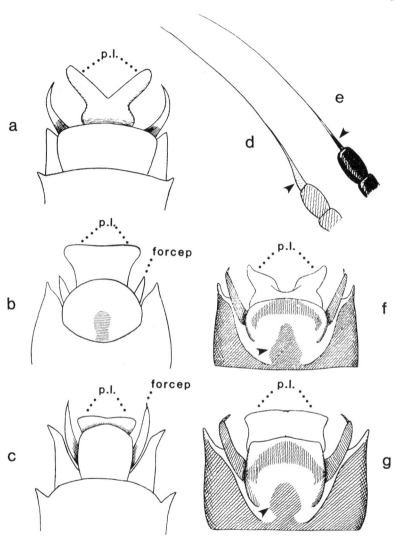

Fig. 35. *Caenis* spp.: male genitalia (ventral) of *a*, *C. rivulorum*; *b*, *C. robusta*, *c*, *C. horaria*; antennae of *d*, *C. luctuosa*; *e*, *C. macrura*; male genitalia (ventral) of *f*, *C. luctuosa*; *g*, *C. macrura*.

ECOLOGY OF ADULTS

It is not known why Ephemeroptera, alone among the winged insects, have two adult stages, the subimago and the imago. One suggestion is that the marked increase in length of the fore legs of the male and of the caudal filaments of both sexes cannot be accomplished in a single moult (Maiorana 1979). It has also been proposed that the two stages have been retained because there has not been the selective pressure on the short-lived adult stage to produce one moult (Schaefer 1975).

Adults do not feed, and live for only a short period that varies in different species from a few hours to about two weeks. Their chief functions are reproduction and dispersal, and their ecology is reviewed under three major headings; emergence and flight period; flight behaviour and mating; fecundity and oviposition behaviour, including egg development.

EMERGENCE AND FLIGHT PERIOD

In order to emerge from the last larval stage, the subimago has to move towards the water surface. This is a critical period for the animal because it is usually vulnerable to aquatic and aerial predators, especially fish and birds. Just prior to emergence, the mature larva becomes more active. In species that emerge during the day, the diel activity pattern of the mature larvae frequently changes from nocturnal to diurnal and the larvae may move on to the upper surfaces of large stones. The time spent in preparation for emergence varies with the species and local conditions, but, once emergence starts, it is completed rapidly, the actual time varying in different species from a few seconds to several minutes.

Most species emerge at the water surface, but several species first leave the water as mature larvae that crawl up sticks, stones, macrophytes or other objects projecting from the water (Table 3). At least one species emerges underwater on the surface of a submerged stone. Although species can be divided into three groups on the basis of the place of emergence, the observations of different authors working on the same species do not always agree and therefore some species have to be placed in more than one group (Table 3). In all species, the epicuticle on the dorsal surface

TABLE 3. EMERGENCE BEHAVIOUR OF SUBIMAGINES OF EPHEMEROPTERA OCCURRING IN BRITAIN

1. Emergence takes place on the surface of the water.
   Baetis muticus (2), *B. rhodani* (2), *Baetis* spp. (3,10), *Cloeon dipterum* (3,8,12), *C. simile* (2), *Rhithrogena semicolorata* (10), *Heptagenia lateralis* (10), *Ecdyonurus venosus* (10), *Ephemerella ignita* (10), *Leptophlebia vespertina* (6), *Habrophlebia fusca* (10,12), *Potamanthus luteus* (10), *Ephemera danica* (2,4,7,8).

2. Emergence takes place partly or entirely out of the water on a stick, stone, or stem of a macrophyte.
   Siphlonurus lacustris (1,12), *Siphlonurus* sp. (2), *Ecdyonurus* spp. (4,9), *Leptophlebia vespertina* (6,10,11), *Paraleptophlebia submarginata* (10), *Habrophlebia fusca* (3,8,10), *Potamanthus luteus* (10), *Ephemera danica* (7).

3. Emergence takes place on a stone beneath the surface of the water.
   Heptagenia lateralis (5).

References: 1, Drenkelfort 1910; 2, Harris 1956; 3, Heiner 1915; 4, Humpesch unpublished; 5, Kimmins 1941; 6, Kjellberg 1972; 7, Percival & Whitehead 1926; 8, Pleskot 1957; 9, Rawlinson 1939; 10, Schoenemund 1930; 11, Tiensuu 1935; 12, Ulmer 1924.

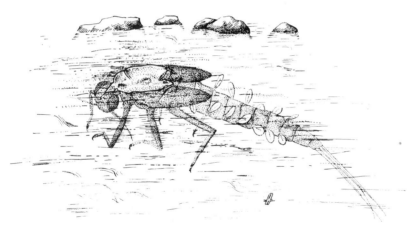

Fig. 36. Floating cast skin of a larva of *Baetis rhodani* after the subimago has emerged (original drawing by M. Mizzaro).

of first the thorax and then the head of the mature larva splits apart. The subimago emerges and erects its wings simultaneously. The cast skins (exuviae) are frequently seen floating on the water surface during the emergence period (fig. 36).

Most species emerge during daylight, often around midday, but several species emerge at dawn or dusk and at least one species can emerge at both dusk and dawn (Table 4). Even in the continuous daylight of the arctic summer, *Baetis muticus* and *Heptagenia sulphurea* maintained a diel rhythm of emergence with a distinct afternoon peak (Thomas 1970). Although these observations suggest that there is an endogenous component to the

TABLE 4. EMERGENCE PATTERN OF SUBIMAGINES OF EPHEMEROPTERA OCCURRING IN BRITAIN

1. Emergence takes place during daylight.
   Siphlonurus alternatus (7), *S. lacustris* (2,5,17b), *Ameletus inopinatus* (16,17b), *Baetis atrebatinus* (10), *B. fuscatus* (10), *B. muticus* (5,10,17b), *B. niger* (3,10), *B. rhodani* (3,4,5,8,10,15,17b), *B. scambus* (3,5,10), *B. vernus* (10), *Baetis* spp. (14), *Centroptilum luteolum* (10,13,17a), *Cloeon dipterum* (7,10,12,16), *C. simile* (6,12), *Cloeon* spp. (14), *Rhithrogena germanica* (10), *R. semicolorata* (5,13,15,16), *Heptagenia sulphurea* (4,17b), *Ecdyonurus venosus* (5,15), *Ecdyonurus* spp. (8), *Leptophlebia marginata* (12,17b,18), *L. vespertina* (11,12,13), *Paraleptophlebia submarginata* (17b), *Ephemera danica* (13,17a), *Ephemerella ignita* (3,5,10,13,15,17a), *Caenis rivulorum* (4).

2. Emergence takes place at dawn.
   Ephemera vulgata (14), *Caenis luctuosa* (9b, 13).

3. Emergence takes place at dusk.
   Baetis atrebatinus (10), *B. rhodani* (4), *B. vernus* (10), *Cloeon dipterum* (1), *Heptagenia lateralis* (14), *H. sulphurea* (4), *Ecdyonurus venosus* (16), *Ecdyonurus* spp. (14), *Potamanthus luteus* (16), *Ephemera vulgata* (18), *Ephemerella ignita* (4,14,16,17a), *Caenis horaria* (7,8,9a,b,12), *C. rivulorum* (9a).

4. Emergence takes place at dawn and dusk.
   Rhithrogena semicolorata (14).

References: 1, Baume 1909; 2, Drenkelfort 1910; 3, Elliott 1967b; 4, Elliott & Corlett 1972; 5, Elliott & Minshall 1968; 6, Harris 1956; 7, Hirvenoja 1964; 8, Humpesch unpublished; 9, Kimmins a 1943a, b, 1943b; 10, Kite 1962; 11, Kjellberg 1972; 12, Morgan & Waddell 1961; 13, Müller-Liebenau 1960; 14, Pleskot & Pomeisl 1952; 15, Riederer 1981; 16, Schoenemund 1930; 17, Thomas a 1969, b 1970; 18, Wesenberg-Lund 1913.

emergence rhythm, other workers have found that the rhythm can be modified or suppressed. For example, a total illumination less than 320 cal cm^{-2} day^{-1} (equivalent to a mean light-intensity of *c*. 3 lux) caused a reduction in the emergence rate of *Baetis rhodani* (Riederer 1981), and the normal diurnal rhythm of emergence in the non-British *Baetis alpinus* was disturbed by constant light and depressed by constant darkness (Humpesch 1971). Variations in the diel cycle of water temperature and light intensity probably affect the amplitude of the periodicity in the diel emergence rhythm and these variations may partially explain why observations of different authors working on the same species do not always agree (Table 4). The various factors affecting emergence have been reviewed by Riederer (1981) and his summary of the more important factors is presented in fig. 37.

Although the diel emergence rhythm of male and female subimagines is usually synchronous, there may occasionally be an excess of males or females at the onset of emergence on some days (Riederer 1981; Brittain 1982).

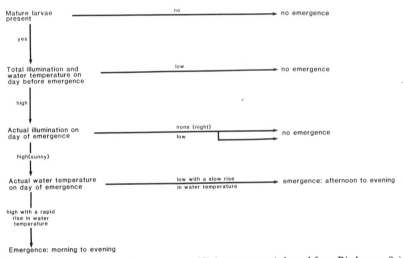

Fig. 37. Factors affecting the emergence of Ephemeroptera (adapted from Riederer 1981).

After emergence, the subimago flies away from the water and usually shelters amongst vegetation where it moults to the imago stage. The subimago first spreads its fore wings sideways, then a split appears medially on the dorsal surface of first the thorax and then the head. The head, thorax and legs of the imago emerge through this split, and the imago usually uses its legs to pull the abdomen and caudal filaments free from

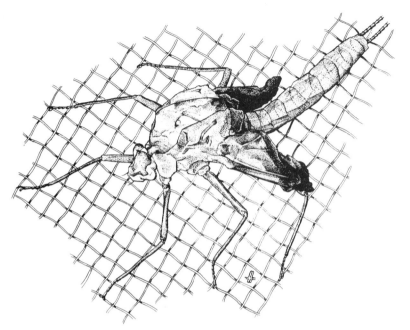

Fig. 38.   Cast skin of the female subimago of *Baetis* sp. after the imago has emerged (original drawing by M. Mizzaro).

the skin of the subimago (Frontispiece).   These cast skins (exuviae) are frequently found on the undersides of leaves on vegetation near the water.   They usually retain all the external features of the subimago except the wings (fig. 38).

The moult to the imago stage may occur within a few minutes after the subimago comes to rest, for example in *Caenis* spp., or it may not occur for two or three days.   This period frequently decreases with increasing air temperature (Thomas 1969; Humpesch 1971).   An example of this relationship is provided by a re-analysis of data for *Leptophlebia marginata* (fig. 39).   The relationship is well described by a power law but unfortunately there is no comparable information for other species.

The final moult of the subimago to the imago is not found in females of some non-British species of Ephemeroptera in the families Behningiidae, Polymitarcyidae and Palingeniidae (e.g. Schoenemund 1930; Edmunds 1956; Peters & Peters 1977; Soldan 1979).   As these females are mature

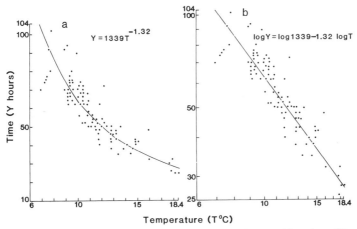

Fig. 39. Relationship between the time required (Y hours) for the subimagines of *Leptophlebia marginata* to emerge and the arithmetic mean air temperature (T °C) in the field (original data from Thomas 1969): *a*, on arithmetic scale with curvilinear regression line; *b*, on log/log scale with linear regression line (note that there were replicates for some readings and the number of replicates for each point can be found in Thomas 1969).

in the subimago stage whilst the corresponding males moult to the imago stage, males usually emerge well before females in these species.

As adult Ephemeroptera live for only a short period of time, the period over which flying adults can be found in any one year is similar to the emergence period. The flight periods of the British species are summarized in Table 5 but adults will rarely be found at any one locality for the whole of this period. Adults are usually present in the warmer months (April to September) but are occasionally found in colder months. For example, Kite (1962) recorded the emergence of five species (*Baetis atrebatinus, B. scambus, B. vernus, Centroptilum luteolum, Ephemerella ignita*) in January, and Elliott (1967b) caught adults of *B. rhodani* in every month.

The emergence and flight periods of widely distributed species frequently vary with both latitude and altitude. For example, the flight period of *Leptophlebia* spp. is progressively later in the year as the distance from the north pole decreases, and the start of emergence is also delayed as altitude increases (Pleskot 1951; Brittain 1972, 1974; Kjellberg 1972). Marked differences may also occur within a relatively short distance. For example, *Ecdyonurus torrentis* had a flight period of three months in the upper reaches and only one month in the lower reaches of a small river, whilst *Ephemerella ignita* emerged throughout four months in the lower

TABLE 5. SUMMARY OF INFORMATION ON FLIGHT PERIODS OF EPHEMEROPTERA OCCURRING IN BRITAIN

Dun = Subimago, Spinner = Imago

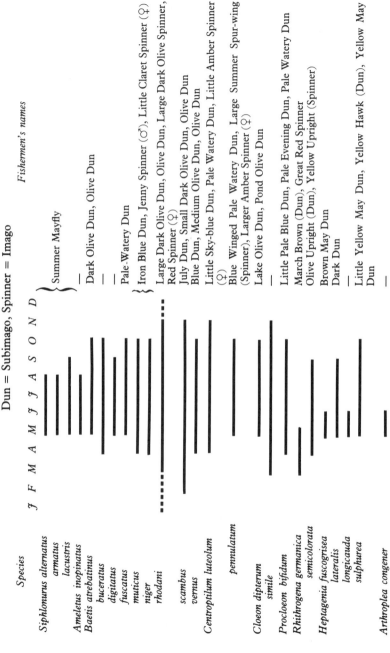

Species	Fishermen's names
Siphlonurus alternatus	⎫
armatus	⎬ Summer Mayfly
lacustris	⎭
Ameletus inopinatus	
Baetis atrebatinus	Dark Olive Dun, Olive Dun
buceratus	—
digitatus	Pale-Watery Dun
fuscatus	Iron Blue Dun, Jenny Spinner (♂), Little Claret Spinner (♀)
muticus	⎫ Large Dark Olive Dun, Olive Dun, Large Dark Olive Spinner, Red Spinner (♀)
niger	⎬ July Dun, Small Dark Olive Dun, Olive Dun
rhodani	⎭ Blue Dun, Medium Olive Dun, Olive Dun
scambus	Little Sky-blue Dun, Pale Watery Dun, Little Amber Spinner (♀)
vernus	
Centroptilum luteolum	Blue Winged Pale Watery Dun, Large Summer Spur-wing (Spinner), Larger Amber Spinner (♀)
pennulatum	Lake Olive Dun, Pond Olive Dun
Cloeon dipterum	
simile	Little Pale Blue Dun, Pale Evening Dun, Pale Watery Dun
Procloeom bifidum	March Brown (Dun), Great Red Spinner
Rhithrogena germanica	Olive Upright (Dun), Yellow Upright (Spinner)
semicolorata	Brown May Dun
Heptagenia fuscogrisea	Dark Dun
lateralis	
longicauda	Little Yellow May Dun, Yellow Hawk (Dun), Yellow May Dun
sulphurea	
Arthroplea congener	—

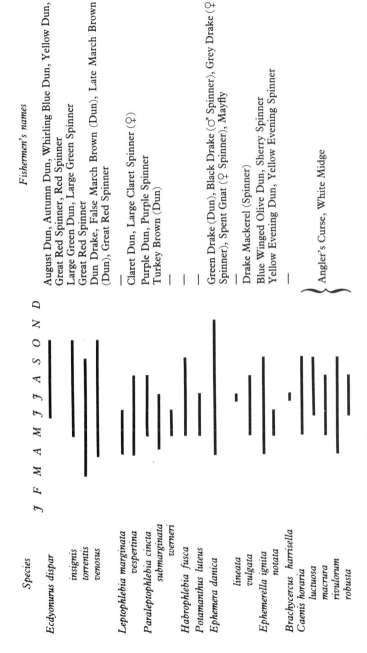

Species   J F M A M J J A S O N D   *Fishermen's names*

Ecdyonurus dispar — August Dun, Autumn Dun, Whirling Blue Dun, Yellow Dun, Great Red Spinner, Red Spinner
insignis — Large Green Dun, Large Green Spinner
torrentis — Great Red Spinner
venosus — Dun Drake, False March Brown (Dun), Late March Brown (Dun), Great Red Spinner

Leptophlebia marginata — Claret Dun, Large Claret Spinner (♀)
vespertina
Paraleptophlebia cincta — Purple Dun, Purple Spinner
submarginata — Turkey Brown (Dun)
werneri — —

Habrophlebia fusca — —
Potamanthus luteus — —
Ephemera danica — Green Drake (Dun), Black Drake (♂ Spinner), Grey Drake (♀ Spinner), Spent Gnat (♀ Spinner), Mayfly
lineata
vulgata — Drake Mackerel (Spinner)
Ephemerella ignita — Blue Winged Olive Dun, Sherry Spinner
notata — Yellow Evening Dun, Yellow Evening Spinner

Brachycercus harrisella
Caenis horaria
luctuosa
macrura
rivulorum   } Angler's Curse, White Midge
robusta

reaches and in only two months in the upper reaches of the same river (Wise 1980).

When several species occur together, they frequently follow a definite order of emergence so that each species emerges in maximum numbers at a different time (see for example, Brittain 1978, 1979, 1980; Thibault 1971; Macan 1965, 1981). This order of succession usually remains constant in each year, even though the actual emergence and flight periods of each species may vary considerably from year to year.

Various factors have been suggested as having an influence on emergence and flight periods, and these include temperature, photoperiod, wind speed and direction, humidity and precipitation (see review by Brittain 1982). Of all these factors, temperature has been the most frequently studied and may have a direct or an indirect effect. An example of the direct effect is *Ecdyonurus dispar*; the larvae grow faster and emergence occurs earlier at higher temperatures than at lower temperatures (Humpesch 1981). Another example is *Rhithrogena semicolorata*, whose flight period ends when the air temperature reaches about 16°C and remains at or above that value for two weeks or longer (Macan 1960). An example of an indirect effect is provided by the non-British *Habroleptoides modesta*. This species must be flying before a water temperature of about 18°C is reached or it will die because of the effect of the high temperature on the oxygen requirements of the mature larvae (Pleskot 1953; Hilmy 1962). Although temperature frequently appears to affect emergence and flight periods, this is not always true. For example, after an exceptionally severe winter, the emergence and flight periods of several species of Plecoptera were markedly later in a small stony stream but no similar retardation was shown by the Ephemeroptera (Elliott 1967b). In a study of emergence patterns in a large river, a thermal discharge from a power station had no obvious effects on the onset or progress of emergence of either Ephemeroptera or Trichoptera (Langford 1975). There is clearly a need for more experimental work on temperature effects, especially in relation to other factors that may affect emergence and flight periods.

FLIGHT BEHAVIOUR AND MATING

Only the males form swarms except in the Caenidae where both sexes participate. The purpose of swarming is to bring the sexes together because eventually the females fly into the male swarm and mate. Swarming males are positively orientated to the wind and also to terrain markers such as vegetation areas, shoreline and trees.

The swarming flight is usually characterized by a peculiar rise and fall of the fly, where the body hangs obliquely as the fly spins forward and upward in a straight line; the fore legs project in front of the head, the cerci spread out behind, and the wings vibrate so rapidly that they are scarcely visible. Spinning is interrupted by short horizontal flights. Swarming may take place over the water itself (e.g. *Siphlonurus*, *Centroptilum*, *Rhithrogena*, *Heptagenia*, *Ecdyonurus*), over the shore area (e.g. *Heptagenia*, *Caenis*), or even remote from the water (e.g. *Baetis*, *Cloeon*, *Leptophlebia*, *Ephemera*). The swarms are to be found at different heights: *Centroptilum luteolum* swarms just over the surface of the water, several *Baetis* spp. swarm high up over the trees. As the swarms are mostly found at similar places, it has been assumed that each species orientates visually to a swarm marker. Savolainen (1978) showed that these markers were either light-coloured horizontal markers (*Siphlonurus*, *Baetis*, *Leptophlebia*, *Caenis*), extensive vegetation (*Leptophlebia*, *Ephemera*), the shoreline (*Centroptilum*, *Heptagenia*, *Ecdyonurus*), or vertical markers such as trees, bushes or buildings (*Leptophlebia*, *Caenis*).

Swarming usually occurs in daylight but some species swarm at dusk or dawn (Table 6). Once again there is some disagreement between workers as to the exact swarming times of some species. Several workers have suggested that there is a diel periodicity in the swarming, but the mechanisms controlling this swarming are poorly known. Pleskot & Pomeisl (1952) observed that the dawn swarming of *Caenis luctuosa* became gradually later according to the daily change in sunrise and they therefore suggested that light intensity controlled the timing of swarming. Such a control has been assumed by various authors and critical light intensities are given for several species (summarized by Savolainen 1978). Therefore the disagreements in Table 6 are probably artefacts due to recording the time instead of the light intensity at which swarming occurs. Other factors such as wind, air temperature and humidity probably act synergistically and may reduce or inhibit swarming, but their real influence and their threshold and/or optimal values are poorly known. None of these observations is supported by experimental work. Savolainen (1978) stresses the point that several aspects of swarming cannot be accounted for by the factors mentioned above, and therefore there may also be an endogenous rhythm. It is not known if swarming is a form of gregarious behaviour where individuals react to one another in order to remain in the swarm or whether each swarmer orientates individually to a marker.

Females fly into the male swarms and mating occurs almost immediately, usually in flight. The male grasps the female from beneath by curving his long fore legs back over her thorax and using his forceps to grasp her abdomen (fig. 40). Copulation occurs whilst the pair slowly descend to the ground and is usually completed before they reach the ground. The copulation period is therefore very short and the pair soon separate. The females usually start to lay their eggs soon after copulation.

TABLE 6. SWARMING PATTERN OF MALES OF EPHEMEROPTERA OCCURRING IN BRITAIN

1.   Swarming takes place during daylight
1.1   Morning only
Siphlonurus spp. (10), *Baetis* spp. (1), *Cloeon simile* (3), *Leptophlebia* spp. (10), *Paraleptophlebia submarginata* (8,14), *Ephemerella ignita* (14).

1.2   Morning, midday, afternoon
Siphlonurus lacustris (2), *Baetis atrebatinus* (3,6), *B. buceratus* (3), *B. muticus* (3,8), *B. rhodani* (3), *B. scambus* (3), *B. vernus* (3), *Centroptilum luteolum* (3), *Cloeon* spp. (1,11), *Rhithrogena semicolorata* (3,8,10), *Heptagenia fuscogrisea* (3,13), *Ecydonurus venosus* (3,8,12,13,14), *Leptophlebia marginata* (13), *L. vespertina* (8,13,15), *Paraleptophlebia cincta* (3), *Ephemera danica* (3,7,8,9,10,14), *E. vulgata* (7,8,10,13), *Ephemerella* spp. (11).

1.3   Afternoon only
Ameletus inopinatus (14), *Baetis* spp. (1), *Cloeon dipterum* (14), *C. simile* (3,7), *Heptagenia sulphurea* (15), *Ecdyonurus dispar* (3), *E. insignis* (3,8), *Paraleptophlebia submarginata* (8), *Ephemerella ignita* (3,8,15).

2.   Swarming takes place at dawn
Siphlonurus alternatus (13), *S. lacustris* (14), *Procloeon bifidum* (3), *Caenis luctuosa* (5a,b,7,8,10), *C. macrura* (5c), *Caenis* spp. (3).

3.   Swarming takes place at dusk
Siphlonurus alternatus (3), *S. lacustris* (3), *Siphlonurus* spp. (10), *Baetis fuscatus* (15), *B. niger* (8), *Centroptilum luteolum* (8,13), *C. pennulatum* (8), *Cloeon dipterum* (4), *Procloeon bifidum* (3), *Heptagenia sulphurea* (3), *Heptagenia* spp. (10), *Ecdyonurus insignis* (14), *Ecdyonurus* spp. (10), *Leptophlebia vespertina* (14), *Leptophlebia* spp. (10), *Paraleptophlebia submarginata* (14), *Ephemera danica* (15), *E. vulgata* (13,16), *Ephemerella ignita* (10,14,15), *E. notata* (3), *Caenis horaria* (7,13,15), *Caenis* spp. (3).

References: 1, Bogoescu 1939; 2, Drenkelfort 1910; 3, Harris 1956; 4, Heiner 1915; 5, Kimmins a 1943a, b 1943b, c 1972; 6, Kite 1962; 7, Malzacher 1973; 8, Müller-Liebenau 1960; 9, Percival & Whitehead 1926; 10, Pleskot 1957; 11, Pleskot & Pomeisl 1952; 12, Rawlinson 1939; 13, Savolainen 1978; 14, Schoenemund 1930; 15, Tiensuu 1935; 16, Wesenberg-Lund 1913.

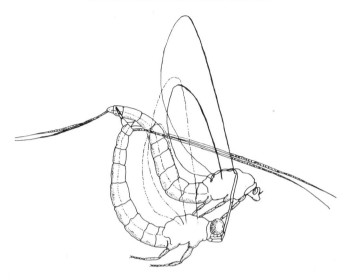

Fig. 40. Mating couple in flight; male below the female (adapted from a drawing in Brinck 1957).

The sex ratio of adult Ephemeroptera may vary between species and between populations of the same species. It is usually about 1:1 (Hirvenoja 1964; Illies 1971, 1980; Sandrock 1978; Röser 1980). Such a ratio was also recorded for many species in an English river, but a ratio of 3♀:1♂ was also recorded for *Baetis buceratus*, *B. fuscatus*, *B. muticus*, *B. rhodani* and *Cloeon dipterum* in the latter river (Langford 1975), and a ratio of 2♀:3♂ was found for *Ephemera danica* in a Swedish stream (Svensson 1977). Information on the number of chromosomes in Ephemeroptera species occurring in Britain is sparse (Table 7).

TABLE 7. NUMBER OF CHROMOSOMES IN EPHEMEROPTERA OCCURRING IN BRITAIN
(2n = diploid number)

	2n +	male/female		Reference
Baetis rhodani	8	XY	XX	1
B. vernus	8	XY	XX	1
Cloeon dipterum	8	XY	XX	2b,3
Ecdyonourus dispar	18	XY	XX	4
Ephemera danica	10	XO	XX	2a,4
Ephemerella ignita	14	(?)XY	XX	4
Caenis horaria	6	XO	—	4

References: 1, Bohle 1969; 2, Wolf a 1946, b 1960; 3, Kiauta & Mol 1977; 4, Mol 1978.

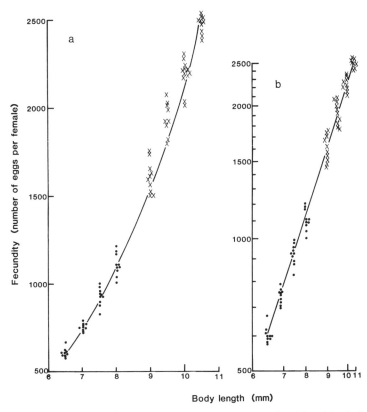

Fig. 41. Relationship between fecundity (number of eggs per female) and body length (mm) of *Baetis rhodani*, using data from a summer generation (●) and a winter generation (×): *a*, on arithmetic scale with curvilinear regression line; *b*, on log/log scale with linear regression line.

FECUNDITY, OVIPOSITION BEHAVIOUR AND EGG DEVELOPMENT

Fecundity is usually defined as the number of ripening eggs in the female prior to oviposition. Although information on fecundity is available for many of the British species (Table 8), most of this information is for only a few females of each species and usually the size of the females is not given. This is unfortunate because fecundity increases with increasing size of the female (fig. 41). The relationship between fecundity (Y eggs

TABLE 8. FECUNDITY OF EPHEMEROPTERA OCCURRING IN BRITAIN

1. Up to *c.* 1200 eggs per female
   Baetis fuscatus (13), *B. niger* (5), *Cloeon dipterum* (5,14), *Leptophlebia marginata* (3), *L. vespertina* (3,10), *Paraleptophlebia submarginata* (7,11,13), *Habrophlebia fusca* (7), *Ephemerella ignita* (2b,5,6b,8,11), *Caenis horaria* (5), *C. luctuosa* (5), *C. macrura* (5).

2. Up to *c.* 2500 eggs per female
   Siphlonurus lacustris (3,5), *Baetis muticus* (5,11), *Centroptilum luteolum* (5,11), *C. pennulatum* (5), *Heptagenia lateralis* (5), *Ecdyonurus dispar* (5,9), *Leptophlebia vespertina* (5,7,11,13).

3. 2000-3500 eggs per female
   Cloeon simile (4,5), *Ecdyonurus insignis* (9), *Ephemera danica* (15).

4. Up to *c.* 4500 eggs per female
   Baetis rhodani (1,2a,6a,8).

5. Up to *c.* 6000 eggs per female
   Ecdyonurus venosus (9,12), *Ephemera danica* (5,8,11), *E. vulgata* (11).

6. 5000-8300 eggs per female
   Ecdyonurus torrentis (9), *Ephemera danica* (16).

References: 1, Benech 1972b; 2, Bohle a 1969, b 1972; 3, Brittain 1980; 4, Davidson 1956; 5, Degrange 1960; 6, Elliott a 1972, b 1978; 7, Grandi 1960; 8, Harris 1956; 9, Humpesch unpublished; 10, Kjellberg 1972; 11, Landa 1969; 12, Rawlinson 1939; 13, Schoenemund 1930; 14, Soldan 1979; 15, Whelan 1980; 16, Wright, Hiley & Berrie 1981.

per female) and body length (L mm from front of head to tip of abdomen) has been shown to be well described by the power law ($Y = aL^b$ where a and b are constants). Such a relationship has been found for *Baetis rhodani* (Benech 1972b; Elliott & Humpesch 1980; see fig. 41), and for the North American species *Leptophlebia cupida* (Clifford 1970; Clifford & Boerger 1974), *Hexagenia limbata* (calculated from data in Hunt 1951), and *Ephemera simulans* (calculated from data in Britt 1962). The value of b in these studies is close to 3 (range 2·66–3·04). Sweeney (1978) found that fecundity was a linear function of dry body weight in three North American species.

When there is a long flight period (Table 5), the females that emerge early are larger and more fecund than those that emerge later, e.g. *Baetis rhodani* (Benech 1972b; see also fig. 41), *Ecdyonurus venosus* (U. H. Humpesch, unpublished). Sweeney & Vannote (1978) have proposed that similar changes in North American species are due chiefly to temperature. This apparently affects adult size and fecundity by altering the larval growth rate as well as the timing and rate of adult tissue development.

Several workers have described the morphology of the eggs (Degrange 1960; Koss 1968; Kopelke & Müller-Liebenau 1981a, b, 1982; Malzacher 1982; and review by Hinton 1981). The eggs of most species have a length of between 150 and 200 μm and a width of between 90 and 150 μm, but the eggs of the larger species may be 250–300 μm long by 150–200 μm wide. Various attachment structures ensure that the eggs adhere to submerged objects or the substratum. The eggs of some species have an external adhesive layer that swells on contact with water, whilst eggs of other species have their surface covered with sucker-like discs or plates, adhesive projections or coiled or uncoiled threads that often have terminal knobs. Species in a third group have polar caps at one or both ends of their eggs. Each polar cap swells on contact with water and releases a large number of threads with terminal knobs.

In streams and rivers, most females fly in an upstream direction before laying their eggs. It has been proposed by several workers that the recolonization of headwater areas by ovipositing females compensates for the downstream drifting of eggs and larvae (Thomas 1975; Lavandier 1982; and review by Müller 1982). Other workers have concluded that such movements occur over short distances and the direction of flight is determined largely by the wind (Elliott 1967a; Waters 1969; Bishop & Hynes 1969; Keller 1975; Gyselman 1980), or that an upstream movement occurs in some species but not in other species of Ephemeroptera in the same stream (Bird & Hynes 1981). In some *Ephemerella* spp., the females form swarms before laying their eggs and these swarms start to form at dusk (Pleskot & Pomeisl 1952).

The eggs are always laid in the water, but they hatch immediately on contact with water in the ovoviviparous *Cloeon dipterum*. Information on oviposition behaviour in the British species is summarized in Table 9. The following five basic types of oviposition behaviour occur but there is some disagreement over the classification of some species.

1. Female goes underwater and eggs are laid on the substratum
Baetis rhodani belongs to this category (Elliott 1972). The female lands on a partially submerged stone in rapidly flowing water, folds her wings along the abdomen, then walks under the water and searches for a suitable oviposition site, usually on the underside of the stone. She always faces the current and swings her abdomen from side to side until a row of eggs is laid in an arc. The female moves slowly forward and thus lays contiguous rows of eggs to form a flat semicircular plate with its concave edge facing the current (fig. 42a). When oviposition ceases, the female may walk out of the water and fly away, but she is usually swept away downstream.

TABLE 9. OVIPOSITION BEHAVIOUR OF EPHEMEROPTERA OCCURRING IN BRITAIN (? indicates that the observation is doubtful)

1. Female goes underwater and eggs laid on substratum
   Baetis fuscatus (11,14b), ?*B. muticus* (6,14a), *B. rhodani* (1,2,4a,6,12), *B. scambus* (1), *B. vernus* (2).

2. Female rests on stone above water and eggs laid on substratum underwater
   ?*Rhithrogena semicolorata* (11), *Ecdyonurus dispar* (7), ?*E. venosus* (16).

3. Female flies down to water surface and eggs released in one mass
   Siphlonurus armatus (14b), *S. lacustris* (16), *Centroptilum luteolum* (6,9), ?*Paraleptophlebia submarginata* (16), ?*Ephemera danica* (6), *Ephemerella ignita* (see refs. in 4b), *E. notata* (6).

4. Female flies down to water surface and eggs released in batches
   Baetis fuscatus (6,16), *B. muticus* (5,12), *Cloeon simile* (3b), *Rhithrogena germanica* (13), *R. semicolorata* (4c,8,11,13,16), *Heptagenia sulphurea* (6,13), *Ecdyonurus insignis* (16), *E. torrentis* (4c), *E. venosus* (14b,15,16), *Leptophlebia vespertina* (10,16), *Habrophlebia fusca* (16), *Ephemera danica* (3b,14a), *E. vulgata* (11,16), *Caenis macrura* (11).

5. Ovoviviparous species
   Cloeon dipterum (see refs in 3a).

References: 1, Benech 1972a; 2, Bohle 1969; 3, Degrange a 1959, b 1960; 4, Elliott a 1972, b 1978, c unpublished; 5, Gillies 1950; 6, Harris 1956; 7, Humpesch unpublished; 8, Humpesch & Elliott 1980; 9, Kimmins 1972; 10, Kjellberg 1972; 11, Landa 1969; 12, Macan 1957; 13, Mosely 1938; 14, Percival & Whitehead a 1926, b 1928; 15, Rawlinson 1939; 16, Schoenemund 1930.

Only *Baetis* spp. are known to show this type of behaviour but some *Baetis* spp. may lay their eggs in a different way, e.g. *B. muticus* belongs to this group according to Percival & Whitehead (1928) and Harris (1956), but not according to Gillies (1950) and Macan (1957). North American *Baetis* spp. also belong to this type (Edmunds, Jensen & Berner 1976).

2. Female rests on a stone above water, and eggs are laid on the substratum under water
There are no detailed descriptions for British species, but the oviposition behaviour of *Habroleptoides modesta*, a European species absent from Britain, has been described in detail by Pleskot (1953). The females search for stones that are partially submerged and near the banks. When a suitable stone is found, the female walks backwards until the tip of the

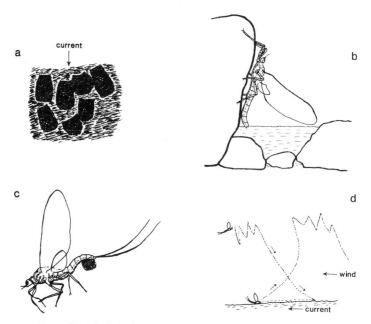

Fig. 42.   a, Eggs of *Baetis rhodani* on a stone;
b, ovipositing female of *Habroleptoides modesta* (adapted from a drawing in Pleskot 1953);
c, female *Ephemerella ignita* carrying ball of eggs;
d, oviposition flight of *Rhithrogena semicolorata*.

abdomen is just under the surface of the water in wet areas between stones and gravel (fig. 42b).   The eggs are laid amongst the gravel but the female is never totally submerged.   The caudal filaments are usually broken off before oviposition starts.

3.   Female flies down to the water surface and eggs are released in a single mass
Ephemerella ignita belongs to this category (Elliott 1978).   The egg mass forms a spherical greenish ball that is carried at the genital aperture, with the posterior abdominal segments curved downwards and round the ball to hold it in position (fig. 42c).   Eggs are usually laid in fast-flowing and turbulent water, usually where moss is present.   The female flies

upstream and descends to the water surface, releasing the egg ball on contact with the water. After ovipositing, the female usually falls on the water surface. The egg mass separates immediately on entering the water and each egg has a polar anchoring cap that attaches the egg to the substratum.

Species in the genera *Siphlonurus, Centroptilum* and *Ephemerella* are known to show this type of behaviour *Ephemera danica* also belongs to this type according to Harris (1956) but *Ephemera* spp. are placed in the next category by all other authors. North American *Ephemerella* spp. also belong to this type (Edmunds et al. 1976).

4. Female flies down to the water surface and eggs are released in several batches

Rhithrogena semicolorata belongs to this category (Humpesch & Elliott 1980). The female flies upstream and descends to the surface of the water, releasing a few eggs by dipping the tip of her abdomen at intervals whilst flying over the water, or by actually settling on the water surface for short periods (fig. 42*d*). The eggs sink to the bottom and are dispersed over a wide area. After several visits to the water surface, all the eggs are released and the spent female usually falls on the water surface.

Most species belong to this category, including the North American species in the families Heptageniidae, Leptophlebiidae and Ephemeridae (Edmunds et al. 1976).

5. Ovoviviparous species

Cloeon dipterum is the only British species known to be in this category. The females rest for 10-14 days after copulation, and then lay their eggs on the surface of the water. As soon as the eggs come into contact with the water, they hatch and the larvae swim away. Some authors claim that the eggs can hatch inside the abdomen of the female, but this is unlikely (see review by Degrange 1959).

The closely related *C. simile* is not ovoviviparous according to Degrange (1959, 1960). North American species in the genus *Callibaetis* are also ovoviviparous (Edmunds et al. 1976). At present, ovoviviparous species are known only in the family Baetidae.

Until recently, there has been no detailed work on egg development and hatching in the laboratory or the field (see review by Elliott & Humpesch 1980). Information is now available for eleven European species (Humpesch & Elliott 1980), including eight species occurring in Britain (Table 10). Most species hatch within the range 3–21 °C, but *B. rhodani* has a higher upper limit of 25 °C whilst the lower limit is between 4·5 °C (no hatching) and 5·9 °C (4–11% hatching) in *R. semicolorata*. Over 90% of

TABLE 10. INFORMATION ON EGG HATCHING OF EPHEMEROPTERA OCCURRING IN BRITAIN

Approximate temperature range over which eggs hatched, mean values for the maximum percentage of eggs that hatched, equation relating hatching time to temperature, whether or not equation has been tested in the field, and mean number (with 95% CL) of days for 50% of the eggs to hatch at 5°C and 10°C.

Species	T °C	Max % hatched	Equation	Tested in field	Days for 50% hatch at 5°C	at 10°C	Reference
Baetis rhodani	3·0–25·0	99	power-law	yes	66(64–68)	26(25–27)	1,2a,3a
B. vernus	6·8–20·0	>94	not known				2a
Rhithrogena semicolorata	5·9–19·9	28	power-law	yes	154(148–160)	41(40–42)	5
Ecdyonurus dispar (lakes)	3·9–20·3	38	power-law	yes	180(170–191)	52(50–54)	4
(rivers)	4·4–20·1	21	not known				4
E. insignis	8·7–19·9	13	power-law	no	—	48(47–49)	4
E. torrentis	3·9–19·6	29	power-law	no	138(124–154)	39(37–41)	4
E. venosus	3·6–20·6	48	power-law	no	166(157–176)	45(43–47)	4
Ephemerella ignita	5·9–19·8	>90	hyperbola	yes	603(526–744)	134(117–165)	2b,3b

References: 1, Bench, 1972a; 2, Bohle a 1969, b 1972; 3, Elliott a 1972, b 1978; 4, Humpesch 1980a, b 1978; 4, Humpesch & Elliott 1980.

the eggs hatched for the two *Baetis* spp. and *E. ignita*, but less than 50% hatched for *R. semicolorata* and the four *Ecdyonurus* spp. This low hatching success probably occurs in the field and must be taken into account in the interpretation of life cycles and population dynamics. There is a clear relationship between hatching success and water temperature in some species (fig. 43), but not in *Ecdyonurus* spp. The Central European species, *R. loyolaea*, is included in fig. 43 as an example of a species with a very narrow range of temperature for hatching.

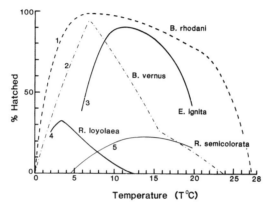

Fig. 43. Comparison of the percentages of eggs hatching at each temperature for European species of Ephemeroptera: 1, *Baetis rhodani* (combined data; Bohle 1969; Elliott 1972; Benech 1972); 2, *B. vernus* (Bohle 1969); 3, *Ephemerella ignita* (Elliott 1978); 4, *Rhithrogena loyolaea*; 5, *R. semicolorata* (Humpesch & Elliott 1980).

The relationship between hatching time (Y days after oviposition or fertilization) and water temperature (T °C) could not be described by an equation in four populations, two of which had a diapause (diapause is a period of suspended development, or growth, with a greatly decreased metabolism) in the egg stage; *Baetis vernus* and one population of *Ephemerella ignita* (Bohle 1969, 1972). In all other populations, the relationship has been well described by a hyperbola or a power law, e.g. British species in Table 10. Both models are summarized by a general equation ($Y = a/(T-t)^b$ where a, b and t are constants). If $t = 0$, then the equation is a two-parameter power law ($Y = aT^{-b}$). If $b = 1$ and t is the threshold temperature at which the development rate is theoretically zero, then the equation is identical to the two-parameter hyperbolic curve ($Y = a/(T-t)$) with the constant, a, equal to the number of degree-days above t °C required for hatching. The general equation has been successfully fitted to

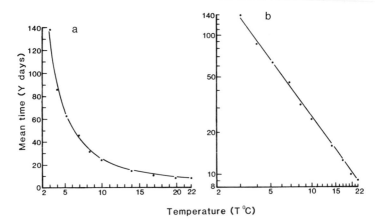

Fig. 44.   Relationship between the mean time required (Y days) for 50% of the eggs of *B. rhodani* to hatch and temperature (T °C) in the laboratory: *a*, on arithmetic scale with curvilinear regression line; *b*, on log/log scale with linear regression line.

data for ten species and fifteen populations of European Ephemeroptera, including seven species occurring in Britain.   A hyperbolic curve was the best model for *E. ignita* whilst a power law was more suitable for the remaining six species (Table 10).   An example of the good fit of the power-law model is given in fig. 44.   The power-law equation was also fitted to data on hatching in the North American species, *Tricorythodes minutus* (Newell & Minshall 1978), but the value of *b* was one and therefore a hyperbolic curve would be an equally good fit.   A logistic equation has been used to describe the relationship between temperature and the days required for the start of hatching in the North American species, *Hexagenia rigida* (Friesen, Flannagan & Lawrence 1979).

The usefulness of the models increases considerably if they can be used to predict the time of hatching in the field.   This has now been tested successfully for six species, including four British species (Table 10). Hatching times vary considerably between species, e.g. values for 50% of eggs to hatch at 5 °C and 10 °C (Table 10).   Hatching times are remarkably similar for different populations of some species (e.g. *Baetis rhodani* from France (Benech 1972a) and England (Elliott 1972), *Ecdyonurus dispar* from two lakes in England (Humpesch 1980a) and *Rhithrogena semicolorata* from two streams in England (Humpesch & Elliott 1980)).   They can also vary considerably between populations of the same species (e.g. *E. dispar* from lakes and rivers (Humpesch 1980a), *E. venosus* from streams in Austria and England (Humpesch 1980a) and *Ephemerella ignita* from streams in France, Germany and England with an obligatory diapause in the eggs of the German population (Thibault 1969; Bohle 1972; Elliott 1978)). These differences may be genuine but it is also possible that the work was on different species that were not recognized because of taxonomic inadequacies.

It has also been shown that in two *Ecdyonurus* spp. and one *Rhithrogena* sp., both the hatching time and rate of development are similar for constant and fluctuating temperatures (Humpesch 1982). Once the eggs start to hatch, the period over which most eggs hatch may be remarkably short in some species, e.g. less than ten days for *Rhithrogena* spp., *Baetis rhodani* (if $T > 5\,°C$), and *Ecdyonurus* spp. (if $T > 10\,°C$) (Elliott 1972; Humpesch 1980a; Humpesch & Elliott 1980). Tiny larvae of these species occur over several months and this observation has often been interpreted as an indication of a long hatching period. It is now obvious that this interpretation is incorrect and therefore the most likely explanation is that some larvae grow very slowly after hatching. This is one example of the value of information on hatching times, and it emphasizes the importance of this information for the interpretation of life cycles.

Eggs can also develop parthenogenetically in many species. Parthenogenesis was recorded by Degrange (1960) in twenty-six European species, fourteen of which occur in Britain, namely: *Caenis luctuosa*, *Ephemerella ignita*, *Ecdyonurus insignis*, *E. dispar*, *Heptagenia lateralis*, *H. sulphurea*, *Leptophlebia vespertina*, *Siphlonurus lacustris*, *Centroptilum luteolum*, *C. pennulatum*, *Cloeon simile*, *Baetis niger*, *B. muticus*, *B. scambus*. Hirvenoja (1964) also recorded parthenogenesis in *Cloeon simile*. Humpesch (1980b) found that eggs can develop parthenogenetically in five species of *Ecdyonurus* and two species of *Rhithrogena*, including the British species *E. dispar*, *E. insignis*, *E. torrentis* and *E. venosus*. For the last two species and for the Central European species, *E. picteti*, there were sufficient data to show that the relationship between hatching time and water temperature was well described by a power law. As males are known for all the European species, the parthenogenesis is not obligatory. When comparisons were made between the development of fertilized and unfertilized (parthenogenetic) eggs, the latter took longer to develop and fewer of them hatched (Degrange 1960; Humpesch 1980b). In some species (e.g. *Cloeon simile*) the unfertilized eggs produced only females, whilst in other species (e.g. *Centroptilum luteolum*) males were also produced but only in low numbers.

Parthenogenesis has been confirmed for fourteen North American species (see references in Mingo 1978; Fiance 1978; Bergman & Hilsenhoff 1978) and one South American species (Froehlich 1969). As males are very rare or absent in five of these species, their parthenogenesis may be obligatory.

FISHERMEN'S FLIES

Adult Ephemeroptera and their imitations have been used by fishermen for several centuries, especially in pursuit of fish of the salmonid family. Emerging duns (subimagines) and fully emerged duns of both sexes, female spinners (imagines), and more rarely male spinners, are found in the stomachs of salmonids and often form the predominant item in the diet of older fish. The characteristic folded wings of the emerging dun are usually simulated on the artificial fly by a small portion of feather and the artificial fly is usually fished as a wet fly just below the water surface. In the fully emerged dun, the dull pattern of the wings is often copied by the use of a mottled feather and the artificial fly is fished as a dry fly. The brighter colours of the spinner are usually copied by the use of coloured, non-mottled feathers and a silk-thread binding to simulate the segmented abdomen. This stage and the imitation of the spent female floating on the water are fished as dry flies.

The usual fishermen's names for the British species are listed in Table 5. The chief problem in using these names is that many species have more than one name and the same name is sometimes used for more than one species. However, the table does serve as a guide to the months over which the adults may be found. Table 4 provides guidance for the time of day when the imitation of the emerging dun should be used. Some species, especially those emerging at dusk or dawn, leave the water in large numbers for only a short period of time. Such a synchronized short period of emergence is shown by *Caenis* spp. and may reduce their risk of predation by fish (Mackey 1978). It is perhaps for this reason, together with their small size and problems of identification, that these species are known as the Angler's Curse! Table 6 can be used as a guide to the times of day when male spinners are swarming and Table 9 provides information on the egg-laying behaviour of female spinners.

It is not known why a fish is attracted to an imitation fly but the availability of food is probably just as important as its abundance. For example, salmonids are essentially visual predators, and on a bright sunny day they may be unable to see clearly any duns or spinners at the air–water interface because of the bright background light. Food may therefore be abundant but unavailable until the evening when the fish may start to feed at the surface. Other factors, such as heavy rain, may also impair the vision of the fish at the air–water interface. Water temperature certainly affects both the appetite and the activity of fish, and both low and high temperatures can cause a cessation of feeding (see reviews by Elliott 1977, 1981, 1982).

Fish may also show some selectivity in their choice of food, especially when it is both abundant and readily available (see review by Williams 1980). This specialization is more evident in fish with full stomachs than in those containing few items of food. The task of matching the fly with a suitable imitation is therefore much more difficult when food is scarce and the fish are feeding at random.

ACKNOWLEDGEMENTS

We wish to thank Mrs P. A. Tullett for all her assistance in the preparation of this booklet, and Dr T. T. Macan and Dr D. W. Sutcliffe for their constructive comments, T. I. Furnass for his assistance with the preparation of the illustrations, Dr T. Soldan for supplying specimens, and J. E. M. Horne for editing the manuscript and supervising its conversion to the final booklet. The originals of the drawings by Prof. Mizzaro-Wimmer are in her possession and she should be consulted before they are reproduced elsewhere. The work in England by U. H. Humpesch was supported jointly by the Austrian Academy of Sciences and the Royal Society through a fellowship from the European Science Exchange Programme.

REFERENCES

Baume, W. La (1909). Über die Metamorphose der Ephemeriden. *Sber. Ges. naturf. Freunde Berl.* **3**, 137-53.

Benech, V. (1972a). Étude expérimentale de l'incubation des oeufs de *Baëtis rhodani* Pictet. *Freshwat. Biol.* **2**, 243-52.

Benech, V. (1972b). La fécondité de *Baëtis rhodani* Pictet. *Freshwat. Biol.* **2**, 337-54.

Bergman, E. A. & Hilsenhoff, W. L. (1978). Parthenogenesis in the mayfly genus *Baëtis* (Ephemeroptera:Baëtidae). *Ann. ent. Soc. Am.* **71**, 167-8.

Bird, G. A. & Hynes, H. B. N. (1981). Movements of adult aquatic insects near streams in southern Ontario. *Hydrobiologia*, **77**, 65-9.

Bishop, J. E. & Hynes, H. B. N. (1969). Downstream drift of the invertebrate fauna in a stream ecosystem. *Arch. Hydrobiol.* **66**, 56-90.

Bogoescu, C. (1939). Biologische Beobachtungen an Ephemeropteren. *Int. Congr. Ent. (Berlin)*, **7**, 1032-43.

Bogoescu, C. & Tabacaru, I. (1962). Beiträge zur Kenntnis der Untersuchungs-merkmale zwischen den Gattungen *Ecdyonurus* und *Heptagenia* (Ephemeroptera). *Beitr. Ent.* **12**, 273-91.

Bohle, H. W. (1969). Untersuchungen über die Embryonalentwicklung und die embryonale Diapause bei *Baëtis vernus* Curtis und *Baëtis rhodani* (Pictet) (Baëtidae, Ephemeroptera). *Zool. Jb. Abt. Anat. Ontog. Tiere*, **86**, 493-575.

Bohle, H. W. (1972). Die Temperaturabhängigkeit der Embryogenese und der embryonalen Diapause von *Ephemerella ignita* (Poda) (Insecta, Ephemeroptera). *Oecologia*, **10**, 253-68.

Brinck, P. (1957). Reproductive system and mating in Ephemeroptera. *Opusc. ent.* **22**, 1-37.

Britt, N. W. (1962). Biology of two species of Lake Erie mayflies, *Ephoron album* (Say) and *Ephemera simulans* Walker. *Bull. Ohio biol. Surv. (N.S.)*, **1**, 5, 1-70.

Brittain, J. E. (1972). The life cycles of *Leptophlebia vespertina* (L.) and *L. marginata* (L.) (Ephemeroptera) in Llyn Dinas, North Wales. *Freshwat. Biol.* **2**, 271-7.

Brittain, J. E. (1974). Studies on the lentic Ephemeroptera and Plecoptera of southern Norway. *Norsk ent. Tidsskr.* **21**, 135-54.

Brittain, J. E. (1978). The Ephemeroptera of Øvre Heimdalsvatn. *Holarct. Ecol.* **1**, 239-54.

Brittain, J. E. (1979). Emergence of Ephemeroptera from Øvre Heimdalsvatn, a Norwegian subalpine lake. In *Proc. 2nd int. Conf. Ephemeroptera, Krakow 1975* (ed. K. Pasternak & R. Sowa), 115-23. Warszawa-Kraków.

Brittain, J. E. (1980). Mayfly strategies in a Norwegian subalpine lake. In *Advances in Ephemeroptera biology* (ed. J. F. Flannagan & K. E. Marshall), 179-86. N.Y. Plenum.

Brittain, J. E. (1982). Biology of mayflies. *A. Rev. Ent.* **27**, 119-47.

Chernova, O. A. (1970). On the classification of the fossil and recent Ephemeroptera [In Russian]. *Ent. Obozr.* **49**, 124-45.

Clifford, H. F. (1970). Analysis of a northern mayfly (Ephemeroptera) population, with special reference to allometry of size. *Can. J. Zool.* **48**, 305-16.

Clifford, H. F. (1982). Life cycles of mayflies (Ephemeroptera), with special reference to voltinism. *Quaest. Ent.* **18**, 15-90.

Clifford, H. F. & Boerger, H. (1974). Fecundity of mayflies (Ephemeroptera), with special reference to mayflies of a brown water stream of Alberta, Canada. *Can. Ent.* **106**, 1111-19.

Davidson, A. (1956). A method of counting Ephemeropteran eggs. *Entomologist's mon. Mag.* **92**, 109.

Degrange, C. (1959). L'ovolarviparité de *Cloëon dipterum* (L.) (Ephemeroptera-Baëtidae). *Bull. Soc. ent. Fr.* **64**, 94-100.

Degrange, C. (1960). Recherches sur la reproduction des Éphéméroptères. *Trav. Lab. Piscic. Univ. Grenoble,* **50/51**, 7-193.

Demoulin, G. (1958). Nouveau schéma de classification des Archodonates et des Éphéméroptères. *Bull. Inst. r. Sci. nat. Belg.* **34**, 1-19.

Drenkelfort, H. (1910). Neue Beiträge zur Kenntnis der Biologie und Anatomie von *Siphlurus lacustris* Eaton. *Zool. Jb. Abt. Anat. Ontog. Tiere,* **29**, 527-617.

Eaton, A. E. (1883-1888). A revisional monograph of recent Ephemeridae or mayflies. *Trans. Linn. Soc. Lond. (Zool.)* **3**, 1-352.

Edmunds, G. F. (1956). Exuvation of subimaginal Ephemeroptera in flight. *Ent. News,* **47**, 91-3.

Edmunds, G. F. (1972). Biogeography and evolution of Ephemeroptera. *A. Rev. Ent.* **17**, 21-42.

Edmunds, G. F. (1975). Phylogenetic biogeography of mayflies. *Ann. Mo. bot. Gdn,* **62**, 251-63.

Edmunds, G. F., Jensen, S. L. & Berner, L. (1976). *The mayflies of North and Central America.* Minneapolis. Univ. Minnesota. 330 pp.

Edmunds, G. F. & Traver, J. R. (1954). An outline and reclassification of the Ephemeroptera. *Proc. ent. Soc. Wash.* **56**, 236-40.

Elliott, J. M. (1967a). Invertebrate drift in a Dartmoor stream. *Arch. Hydrobiol.* **63**, 202-37.

Elliott, J. M. (1967b). The life histories and drifting of the Plecoptera and Ephemeroptera in a Dartmoor stream. *J. Anim. Ecol.* **36**, 343-62.

Elliott, J. M. (1972). Effect of temperature on the time of hatching in *Baëtis rhodani* (Ephemeroptera:Baëtidae). *Oecologia,* **9**, 47-51.

Elliott, J. M. (1977). Feeding, metabolism and growth of brown trout. *Rep. Freshwat. biol. Ass.* **45**, 70-7.

Elliott, J. M. (1978). Effect of temperature on the hatching time of eggs of *Ephemerella ignita* (Poda) (Ephemeroptera:Ephemerellidae). *Freshwat. Biol.* **8**, 51-8.

Elliott, J. M. (1981). Some aspects of thermal stress on freshwater teleosts. In *Stress and fish* (ed. A. D. Pickering), 209-45. London. Academic Press.

Elliott, J. M. (1982). The effects of temperature and ration size on the growth and energetics of salmonids in captivity. *Comp. Biochem. Physiol.* **73B**, 81-91.

Elliott, J. M. & Corlett, J. (1972). The ecology of Morecambe Bay. IV. Invertebrate drift into and from the River Leven. *J. appl. Ecol.* **9**, 195-205.

Elliott, J. M. & Humpesch, U. H. (1980). Eggs of Ephemeroptera. *Rep. Freshwat. biol. Ass.* **48**, 41-52.

Elliott, J. M. & Minshall, G. W. (1968). The invertebrate drift in the River Duddon, English Lake District. *Oikos*, **19**, 39-52.

Fiance, S. B. (1978). Effects of pH on the biology and distribution of *Ephemerella funeralis* (Ephemeroptera). *Oikos*, **31**, 332-39.

Friesen, M. K., Flannagan, J. F. & Lawrence, S. G. (1979). Effects of temperature and cold storage on development time and viability of eggs of the burrowing mayfly *Hexagenia rigida* (Ephemeroptera:Ephemeridae). *Can. Ent.* **111**, 665-73.

Froehlich, C. G. (1969). *Caenis cuniana* sp. n., a parthenogenetic mayfly. *Beitr. neotrop. Fauna*, **6**, 103-8.

Gillies, M. T. (1950). Egg laying of olives. *Salm. Trout Mag.* **129**, 106-8.

Grandi, M. (1960). *Ephemeroidea. Fauna d'Italia*, **3**. Bologna. Calderini. 474 pp.

Gyselman, E. C. (1980). The mechanisms that maintain population stability of selected species of Ephemeroptera in a temperate stream. In *Advances in Ephemeroptera biology* (ed. J. F. Flannagan & K. E. Marshall), 309-19. N.Y. Plenum.

Harris, J. R. (1956). *An angler's entomology.* 2nd edn. London. Collins New Naturalist. 268 pp.

Heiner, H. (1915). Zur Biologie und Anatomie von *Cloëon dipterum* L., *Baetis binoculatus* L. und *Habrophlebia fusca* Curt. *Jena. Z. Naturw.* **53**, 289-340.

Hilmy, A. M. (1962). Experimente zur Atmungsphysiologie von Ephemeropteren-Larven. *Int. Congr. Ent. (Vienna)*, **11**, 254-8.

Hinton, H. E. (1981). *Biology of insect eggs.* 3 vols. Oxford. Pergamon. 1-473; 475-778; 779-1125.

Hirvenoja, M. (1964). Studien über die Wasserinsekten in Riihimäki (Südfinnland). IV: Ephemeroptera, Odonata, Hemiptera, Lepidoptera und Coleoptera. *Annls ent. fenn.* **30**, 65-93.

Humpesch, U. H. (1971). Zur Faktorenanalyse des Schlüpfrhythmus der Flugstadien von *Baetis alpinus* Pict. (Baetidae, Ephemeroptera). *Oecologia*, **7**, 328-41.

Humpesch, U. H. (1980a). Effect of temperature on the hatching time of eggs of five *Ecdyonurus* spp. (Ephemeroptera) from Austrian streams and English streams, rivers and lakes. *J. Anim. Ecol.* **49**, 317-33.

Humpesch, U. H. (1980b). Effect of temperature on the hatching time of parthenogenetic eggs of five *Ecdyonurus* spp. and two *Rhithrogena* spp. (Ephemeroptera) from Austrian streams and English rivers and lakes. *J. Anim. Ecol.* **49**, 927-37.

Humpesch, U. H. (1981). Effect of temperature on larval growth of *Ecdyonurus dispar* (Ephemeroptera:Heptageniidae) from two English lakes. *Freshwat. Biol.* **11**, 441-57.

Humpesch, U. H. (1982). Effect of fluctuating temperature on the duration of embryonic development in two *Ecdyonurus* spp. and *Rhithrogena* cf. *hybrida* (Ephemeroptera) from Austrian streams. *Oecologia,* **55**, 285-8.

Humpesch, U. H. & Elliott, J. M. (1980). Effect of temperature on the hatching time of eggs of three *Rhithrogena* spp. (Ephemeroptera) from Austrian streams and an English stream and river. *J. Anim. Ecol.* **49**, 643-61.

Hunt, B. P. (1951). Reproduction of the burrowing mayfly, *Hexagenia limbata* (Serville), in Michigan. *Fla Ent.* **34**, 59-70.

Illies, J. (1968). Ephemeroptera (Eintagsfliegen). *Handb. Zool.* **4** (2), 2, 5, 1-63.

Illies, J. (1971). Emergenz 1969 im Breitenbach. *Arch. Hydrobiol.* **69**, 14-59.

Illies, J. (1980). Ephemeropteren-Emergenz in zwei Lunzer Bächen (1972-1977). *Arch. Hydrobiol.* **90**, 217-29.

Jacob, U. (1974a). Die bisher nachgewiesenen Ephemeropteren der Deutschen Demokratischen Republik. *Ent. Nachr., Dresden*, **18**, 1-7.

Jacob, U. (1974b). Zur Kenntnis zweier *Oxycypha*-Arten Hermann Burmeisters (Ephemeroptera: Caenidae). *Reichenbachia*, **15**, 93-7.

Keller, A. (1975). Die Drift und ihre ökologische Bedeutung. Experimentelle Untersuchung an *Ecdyonurus venosus* (Fabr.) in einem Fliesswassermodell. *Schweiz. Z. Hydrol.* **37**, 294-331.

Kiauta, B. & Mol, A. W. M. (1977). Behaviour of the spermatocyte chromosomes of the mayfly, *Cloeon dipterum* (Linnaeus, 1761) s.l. (Ephemeroptera: Baetidae), with a note on the cytology of the order. *Genen Phaenen*, **19**, 31-9.

Kimmins, D. E. (1941). Under-water emergence of the subimago of *Heptagenia lateralis* (Curtis) (Ephemeroptera). *Entomologist*, **74**, 169-70.

Kimmins, D. E. (1942). Keys to the British species of Ephemeroptera with keys to the genera of the nymphs. *Scient. Publs Freshwat. biol. Ass.* No. 7, 64 pp.

Kimmins, D. E. (1943a). A species of *Caenis* (Ephemeroptera) new to Britain, with notes on the nymphs of some other species. *Entomologist*, **76**, 123-5.

Kimmins, D. E. (1943b). Further notes on *Caenis moesta* Bengtss. (Ephemeroptera). *Entomologist*, **76**, 199-200.

Kimmins, D. E. (1972). A revised key to the adults of the British species of Ephemeroptera with notes on their ecology. *Scient. Publs Freshwat. biol. Ass.* No. 15, 2nd Revised Edn. 74 pp.

Kite, O. W. A. (1962). Notes on the emergence of ephemeropteran subimagines in 1961. *Salm. Trout Mag.* No. 165, 124-31.

Kjellberg, G. (1972). Autekologiska studier oever *Leptophlebia vespertina* (Ephemeroptera) i en mindre skogstjarn 1966-1968. *Ent. Tidskr.* **93**, 1-29.

Klapálek, F. (1909). I. Ephemerida, Eintagsfliegen. In *Die Süsswasserfauna Deutschlands* (ed. A. Brauer). Heft 8, 1-32. Jena. Gustav Fischer.

Kopelke, J.-P. & Müller-Liebenau, I. (1981a). Eistrukturen bei Ephemeroptera und deren Bedeutung für die Aufstellung von Artengruppen am Beispiel der europäischen Arten der Gattung *Baetis* Leach, 1815. Teil II: *rhodani-*, *vernus-* und *fuscatus-*Gruppe. *Spixiana*, **4**, 39-54.

Kopelke, J.-P. & Müller-Liebenau, I. (1981b). Eistrukturen bei Ephemeroptera und deren Bedeutung für die Aufstellung von Artengruppen am Beispiel der europäischen Arten der Gattung *Baetis* Leach, 1815. Teil III: *buceratus-*, *atrebatinus-*, *niger-*, *gracilis-* und *muticus-*Gruppe (Ephemeroptera, Baetidae). *Dt. ent. Z.* **28**, 1-6.

Kopelke, J.-P. & Müller-Liebenau, I. (1982). Eistrukturen bei Ephemeroptera und deren Bedeutung für die Aufstellung von Artengruppen am Beispiel der europäischen Arten der Gattung *Baetis* Leach, 1815, (Insecta: Baetidae). Teil I: *alpinus-*, *lutheri-*, *pavidus-* und *lapponicus-*Gruppe. *Gewäss. Abwäss*, **68/69**, 7-25.

Koss, R. W. (1968). Morphology and taxonomic use of Ephemeroptera eggs. *Ann. ent Soc. Am.* **61**, 696-721.

Landa, V. (1969). *Jepice—Ephemeroptera. Fauna CSSR*, **18**, 349 pp. Praha. Academia.

Langford, T. E. (1975). The emergence of insects from a British river, warmed by power station cooling-water. Pt. II: The emergence patterns of some species of Ephemeroptera, Trichoptera and Megaloptera in relation to water temperature and river flow, upstream and downstream of cooling-water outfalls. *Hydrobiologia*, **47**, 91-133.

Lavandier, P. (1982). Evidence of upstream migration by female adults of *Baetis alpinus* Pict. (Ephemeroptera) at high altitude in the Pyrenees. *Annls Limnol.* **18**, 55-9.

Macan, T. T. (1957). The life histories and migrations of the Ephemeroptera in a stony stream. *Trans. Soc. Br. Ent.* **12**, 129-56.

Macan, T. T. (1960). The effect of temperature on *Rhithrogena semicolorata* (Ephem.) *Int. Revue ges. Hydrobiol. Hydrogr.* **45**, 197-201.

Macan, T. T. (1965). The fauna in the vegetation of a moorland fish pond. *Arch. Hydrobiol.* **61**, 273-310.

Macan, T. T. (1979). A key to the nymphs of the British species of Ephemeroptera with notes on their ecology. *Scient. Publs Freshwat. biol. Ass.* No. 20, 80 pp.

Macan, T. T. (1981). Life histories of some species of *Ecdyonurus* (Ephemeroptera) in the River Lune, north-western England. *Aquat. Ins.* **3**, 225-32.

Mackey, A. P. (1978). Emergence patterns of three species of *Caenis* Stephens (Ephemeroptera: Caenidae). *Hydrobiologia*, **58**, 277-80.

Maiorana, V. C. (1979). Why do adult insects not moult? *Biol. J. Linn. Soc.* **11**, 253-8.

Malzacher, P. (1973). Eintagsfliegen des Bodenseegebietes (Insecta, Ephemeroptera). *Beitr. naturk. Forsch. SüdwDtl.* **32**, 123-42.

Malzacher, P. (1982). Eistrukturen europäischer Caenidae (Insecta, Ephemeroptera). *Stuttg. Beitr. Naturk.* Ser. A, **356**, 1-15.

McCafferty, W. P. & Edmunds, G. F. (1979). The higher classification of the Ephemeroptera and its evolutionary basis. *Ann. ent. Soc. Am.* **72**, 5-12.

Mingo, T. M. (1978). Parthenogenesis in the mayfly *Stenacron interpunctatum frontale* (Burks) (Ephemeroptera:Heptageniidae). *Ent. News*, **89**, 46-50.

Mol, A. W. M. (1978). Notes on the chromosomes of some West European Ephemeroptera. *Chromosome Inf. Ser.* **24**, 10-12.

Morgan, N. C. & Waddell, A. B. (1961). Diurnal variation in the emergence of some aquatic insects. *Trans. R. ent. Soc. Lond.* **113**, 123-34.

Mosely, M. E. (1938). The spinner and its eggs. *Salm. Trout Mag.* **90**, 18-23.

Müller, K. (1982). The colonization cycle of freshwater insects. *Oecologia*, **52**, 202-7.

Müller-Liebenau, I. (1960). Eintagsfliegen aus der Eifel (Insecta, Ephemeroptera). *Gewäss. Abwäss.* **25**, 55-79.

Müller-Liebenau, I. (1969). Revision der europäischen Arten der Gattung *Baetis* Leach, 1815. (Insecta, Ephemeroptera). *Gewäss. Abwäss.* **48/49**, 1-214.

Needham, J. G. (1905). Mayflies and midges of New York. *Bull. N. Y. St. Mus.* 86 (Entomol. 23), 1-352.

Needham, J. G., Traver, J. R. & Hsu, Y.-C. (1935). *The biology of mayflies, with a systematic account of North American species.* N.Y. Ithaca. 759 pp.

Newell, R. L. & Minshall, G. W. (1978). Effect of temperature on the hatching time of *Tricorythodes minutus* (Ephemeroptera:Tricorythidae). *J. Kans. ent. Soc.* **51**, 504-6.

Percival, E. & Whitehead, H. (1926). Observations on the biology of the mayfly, *Ephemera danica* Müll. *Proc. Leeds phil. lit. Soc.* **1**, 136-48.

Percival, E. & Whitehead, H. (1928). Observations on the ova and oviposition of certain Ephemeroptera and Plecoptera. *Proc. Leeds phil. lit. Soc.* **1**, 271-88.

Peters, W. L. & Peters, J. G. (1977). Adult life and emergence of *Dolania americana* in northwestern Florida (Ephemeroptera:Behningiidae). *Int. Revue ges. Hydrobiol. Hydrogr.* **62**, 409-38.

Pleskot, G. (1951). Wassertemperatur und Leben im Bach. *Wett. Leben*, **3**, 129-43.

Pleskot, G. (1953). Zur Ökologie der Leptophlebiiden (Ins., Ephemeroptera). *Öst. zool. Z.* **4**, 45-107.

Pleskot, G. (1957). Fliegen und Fische. *Öst Fisch.* **10**, 101-114.

Pleskot, G. & Pomeisl, E. (1952). Bedeutung der Lichtintensität beim Schlüpfen und bei der Eiablage von aquatischen Insekten, im besonderen von *Torleya belgica*. *Wett. Leben*, Sonderheft 1, 41-7.

Puthz, V. (1977). Bemerkungen über europäische *Siphlonurus*-Arten (Insecta, Ephemeroptera). *Reichenbachia*, **16**, 169-75.

Puthz, V. (1978). Ephemeroptera. In *Limnofauna Europaea*, 2nd edn (ed. J. Illies), 256-63. Stuttgart. Fischer.

Rawlinson, R. (1939). Studies on the life-history and breeding of *Ecdyonurus venosus* (Ephemeroptera). *Proc. zool. Soc. Lond. Series B*, **109**, 377-450.

Riederer, R. A. A. (1981). Die Entags- und Steinfliegenfauna (Ephemeroptera und Plecoptera) im Mittellauf der Töss. Thesis ETH Zürich, 169 pp.

Riek, E. F. (1973). The classification of the Ephemeroptera. In *Proc. 1st int. Conf. Ephemeroptera, Tallahassee, U.S.A. 1970*, (ed. W. L. Peters & J. G. Peters), 160-78. Leiden, Brill.

Röser, B. (1980). Emergenz eines Mittelgebirgsbaches des Vorderwesterwaldes. *Arch. Hydrobiol. (Suppl.)* **58**, 56-96.

Sandrock, F. (1978). Vergleichende Emergenzmessung an zwei Bächen des Schlitzerlandes (Breitenbach und Rohrwiesenbach 1970-1971). *Arch. Hydrobiol. (Suppl.)* **54**, 328-408.

Savolainen, E. (1978). Swarming in Ephemeroptera: the mechanism of swarming and the effects of illumination and weather. *Annls zool. fenn.* **15**, 17-52.

Schaefer, C. W. (1975). The mayfly subimago: a possible explanation. *Ann. ent. Soc. Am.* **68**, 183.

Schoenemund, E. (1930). Eintagsfliegen oder Ephemeroptera. *Tierwelt Dtl.* 19 Teil, 106 pp.

Soldan, T. (1979). The structure and development of the female internal reproductive system in six European species of Ephemeroptera. *Acta ent. bohemoslav.* **76**, 353-65.

Southwood, T. R. E. (1978). *Ecological methods with particular reference to the study of insect populations.* 2nd edn. London. Chapman & Hall. 524 pp.

Sowa, R. (1971). Notes sur quelques *Rhithrogena* Eaton de la collection Esben-Petersen et la redescription de *Rhithrogena germanica* Eaton (Ephemeroptera, Heptageniidae). *Bull. Acad. pol. Sci.* **19**, 485-92.

Sowa, R. (1975a). What is *Cloeon dipterum* (Linnaeus, 1761)? The nomenclatural and morphological analysis of a group of the European species of *Cloeon* Leach (Ephemerida:Baetidae). *Entomologica scand.* **6**, 215-23.

Sowa, R. (1975b). Notes on the European species of *Procloeon* Bengtsson with particular reference to *Procloeon bifidum* (Bengtsson) and *Procloeon ornatum* Tshernova (Ephemerida:Baetidae). *Entomologica scand.* **6**, 107-14.

Svensson, B. S. (1977). Life cycle, energy fluctuations and sexual differentiation in *Ephemera danica* (Ephemeroptera), a stream-living mayfly. *Oikos*, **29**, 78-86.

Sweeney, B. W. (1978). Bioenergetic and developmental response of a mayfly to thermal variation. *Limnol. Oceanogr.* **23**, 461-77.

Sweeney, B. W. & Vannote, R. L. (1978). Size variation and the distribution of hemimetabolous aquatic insects: two thermal equilibrium hypotheses. *Science, N.Y.* **200**, 444-6.

Thibault, M. (1969). Le développement des Éphéméroptères semivoltins et univoltins d'un ruisseau de Pays Basque Français. Doctorat thèse. Univ. Paris. 78 pp.

Thibault, M. (1971). Le développement des Éphéméroptères d'un ruisseau à truites des Pyrénées-Atlantiques, le Lissuraga. *Annls Limnol.* **7**, 53-120.

Thomas, A. G. B. (1975). Éphéméroptères du sud-ouest de la France. 1. Migrations d'imagos à haute altitude. *Annls Limnol.* **11**, 47-66.

Thomas, E. (1969). Zur Tagesperiodik des Schlüpfens von Ephemeropteren und Plecopteren. *Oecologia*, **3**, 230-9.

Thomas, E. (1970). Die Oberflächendrift eines lappländischen Fliessgewässers. *Oikos*, Suppl. 13, 45-64.

Tiensuu, L. (1935). On the Ephemeroptera fauna of Laatokan Karjala (Karelia Ladogensis). *Annls ent. fenn.* **1**, 3-23.

Ulmer, G. (1914). 4. Ordnung: Eintagsfliegen, Ephemeroptera (Agnatha). In *Fauna von Deutschland* (ed. P. Brohmer) Tab. 10, 95-9. Heidelberg. Quelle & Meyer.

Ulmer, G. (1924). Ephemeroptera. Eintagsfliegen. In *Biologie der Tiere Deutschlands*, Teil 34 (ed. P. Schulze). Berlin. Borntraeger. 27 pp.

Ulmer, G. (1929). 6. Ordnung: Eintagsfliegen, Ephemeroptera (Agnatha). *Tierwelt Mitteleur.* **4**, 1-43.

Waters, T. F. (1969). Invertebrate drift – ecology and significance to stream fishes. In *Symposium on salmon and trout in streams*, 121-34. Vancouver, Univ. B.C.

Wesenberg-Lund, C. (1913). Ephemeridae. In *Fortpflanzungsverhältnisse: Paarung und Eiablage der Süsswasserinsekten. Fortschr. naturw. Fortsch.* **8**, 167-72.

Whelan, K. F. (1980). Some aspects of the biology of *Ephemera danica* Müll. (Ephemeridae:Ephemeroptera) in Irish waters. In *Advances in Ephemeroptera biology* (ed. J. F. Flannagan & K. E. Marshall), 187-99. N.Y. Plenum.

Williams, D. D. (1980). Applied aspects of mayfly biology. In *Advances in Ephemeroptera biology* (ed. J. F. Flannagan & K. E. Marshall), 1-17. N.Y. Plenum.

Wise, E. J. (1980). Seasonal distribution and life histories of Ephemeroptera in a Northumbrian river. *Freshwat. Biol.* **10**, 101-11.

Wolf, E. (1946). Chromosomenuntersuchungen an Insekten. *Z. Naturf.* **1**, 108-9.

Wolf, E. (1960). Zur Karyologie der Eireifung und Furchung bei *Cloeon dipterum* L. (Bengtsson) (Ephemerida, Baetidae). *Biol. Zbl.* **79**, 153-98.

Wright, J. F., Hiley, P. D. & Berrie, A. D. (1981). A 9-year study of the life cycle of *Ephemera danica* Müll. (Ephemeridae:Ephemeroptera) in the River Lambourn, England. *Ecol. Ent.* **6**, 321-31.

INDEX

A. SPECIES

Page numbers in **bold** type indicate main key references, those in *italic* type indicate illustrations. Synonyms are shown in parentheses.

B. FISHERMEN'S NAMES

Angler's Curse – see *Caenis horaria*
                    luctuosa
                    macrura
                    rivulorum
                    robusta
August Dun – see *Ecdyonurus dispar*
Autumn Dun – see *Ecdyonurus dispar*

Black Drake (♂ Spinner) – see *Ephemera danica*
Blue Dun – see *Baetis vernus*
Blue Winged Olive Dun – see *Ephemerella ignita*
Blue Winged Pale Watery Dun – see *Centroptilum pennulatum*
Brown May Dun – see *Heptagenia fuscogrisea*

Claret Dun – see *Leptophlebia vespertina*

Dark Dun – see *Heptagenia lateralis*
Dark Olive Dun – see *Baetis atrebatinus*
Drake Mackerel (Spinner) – see *Ephemera vulgata*
Dun Drake – see *Ecdyonurus venosus*

False March Brown (Dun) – see *Ecdyonurus venosus*

Great Red Spinner – see *Rhithrogena germanica*
                            Ecdyonurus dispar
                                      insignis
                                      venosus

SCIENTIFIC PUBLICATIONS